The Cambridge English Course

This book contains the first third of
the complete edition of *The Cambridge
English Course*, Student's Book 2.

2
Student's Book

Michael Swan and Catherine Walter

CAMBRIDGE
UNIVERSITY PRESS

ISBN 0 521 28984 X Student's Book 2

Split edition:
ISBN 0 521 33757 7 Part A
ISBN 0 521 33758 5 Part B
ISBN 0 521 33759 3 Part C

ISBN 0 521 28982 3 Teacher's Book 2
ISBN 0 521 28983 1 Practice Book 2
ISBN 0 521 31626 X Test Book 2
ISBN 0 521 24817 5 Cassette Set 2
ISBN 0 521 30324 9 Student's Cassette 2

Published by the Press Syndicate of the University of Cambridge
The Pitt Building, Trumpington Street, Cambridge CB2 1RP
40 West 20th Street, New York, NY 10011–4211, USA
10 Stamford Road, Oakleigh, Victoria 3166, Australia

© Cambridge University Press 1985, 1986

Complete edition first published 1985
This split edition first published 1986

Seventh printing 1992

Designed by John Youé and Associates, Croydon, Surrey
Typeset by Text Filmsetters Limited, London
Origination by BTA Reprographics Limited, London
Printed in Great Britain by Scotprint Ltd, Musselburgh, Scotland

Authors' acknowledgements

We are grateful to all the people who have helped us with this book. Our thanks to:

The many people whose ideas have influenced our work, including all the colleagues and students from whom we have learnt.

Ruth Gairns, Stuart Redman, Alan Duff, Alan Maley, Mario Rinvolucri and Penny Ur, for specific ideas and exercises we have borrowed.

Those institutions and teachers who were kind enough to work with the Pilot Edition of this course, and whose comments have done so much to shape the final version.

Peter Roach for his expert and sensible help with the phonetic transcription.

John Youé, Jack Wood, Margaret Dodd, Tanya Ball, Alison Pincott, Jane Molineaux, Jason Youé and Helen Lawrence of John Youé and Associates, for their invaluable help in the design and production of the book.

John and Angela Eckersley, and the staff of the Eckersley School of English, Oxford, for making it possible for us to try out the Pilot Edition of the course in their classrooms.

Ken Blissett, John and Rita Peake, Alexandra Phillips, Pat Robbins, Sue Ward, Adrian Webber, Jane and Keith Woods, for agreeing to be questioned within earshot of our microphones.

Mark, for all his help and support.

And finally, to Adrian du Plessis, Peter Donovan, Jeanne McCarten and Peter Ducker of Cambridge University Press, for their creativity, their understanding, and their outstanding professional competence.

Michael Swan   *Catherine Walter*

The authors and publishers would like to thank the following people and institutions for their help in testing the material and for the invaluable feedback which they provided:

The British Council, Thessaloniki, Greece; The British School, Florence, Italy; Australian College of English, Sydney, Australia; University of Berne, Berne, Switzerland; Etudes Pedagogiques de l'Enseignement Secondaire, Geneva, Switzerland; The Bell School, Cambridge; Bell College, Saffron Waldon; Oxford Language Centre, Oxford; The British Institute, Rome, Italy; The Newnham Language Centre, Cambridge; Adult Migrant Education Services, Melbourne, Australia; Communication in Business, Paris, France; Studio School of English, Cambridge; International House, Arezzo, Italy; Grange School, Santiago, Chile; Eurocentre, Cambridge; Gillian Porter-Ladousse, Paris, France; Pauline Bramall, Karlsruhe, W. Germany; College de Saussure, Geneva, Switzerland; Noreen O'Shea, Paris, France; Eurocentre, Brighton; New School of English, Cambridge; Eckersley School, Oxford; Central School of English, London; Anglo-Continental School, Bournemouth; Godmer House School of English, Oxford; School of English Studies, Folkestone; Davies's School of English, London; Oxford Language Centre, Oxford; Regent School, Rome, Italy; Brunswick Education Centre, Victoria, Australia.

Contents

> **Note**
> Page numbering from the complete edition of Student's Book 2 has been retained throughout.

Map of Book 2*

	FUNCTIONS AND SKILLS	NOTIONS, TOPICS AND SITUATIONS
In Unit	Students will learn to	Students will learn to talk about
1	Make introductions; ask for and give information; describe people; listen for specific information.	Themselves and their interests, people's appearance and behaviour.
2	Make commentaries; express doubt and certainty; take part in simple discussions.	Appearance of things; beliefs.
3	Narrate; express past time relations.	Accidents; basic office situations.
4	Describe; compare.	Similarities and differences; people's appearance.
5	Ask for things without knowing the exact word; make and reply to suggestions, requests and offers.	Shopping; household goods; clothes.
6	Predict; speak on the phone; negotiate.	Probability; certainty; the future; appointments.
7	Ask for and give information.	People's experiences and habits; national and local news; duration; changes.
8	Improve scan reading skills; link written texts; explain reasons for a choice; make reverse-charge phone calls.	Travelling to and in Britain and the US; holidays.
9	Ask for and give information; narrate; apologise and accept apologies; make excuses; link written texts.	Emergencies; causation; blame and responsibility.
10	Predict; deduce; describe processes; give instructions.	Conditions and probability; superstitions; cooking.
REVISION 11	Use what they have learnt in different ways.	Employment; they will revise vocabulary.

*This 'map' of the course should be translated into students' language where possible.

VOCABULARY: Students will learn about 1,000 common words and expressions during the course.

GRAMMAR	PHONOLOGY
Students will learn or revise these grammar points	**Students will study these aspects of pronunciation**
Simple present; *be* and *have*; *have got*; adverbs of degree; *like . . . ing*, no article for general meaning.	Hearing unstressed syllables in rapid speech.
Present progressive; contrast between simple present and present progressive.	/ɪ/ and /iː/; pronunciations of *th*.
Regular and irregular past tenses; past progressive; *when-* and *while*-clauses; ellipsis.	Hearing final consonants; pronunciations of the letter *a*.
Comparative and superlative of adjectives; *than* and *as*; relative clauses with *who*; *do* as pro-verb; compound adjectives.	Decoding rapid speech; stress, rhythm and linking.
At a + shop; *a thing with a . . .*; *a thing for . . . ing*; modal verbs; infinitive with and without *to*.	Rhythm and stress; /eɪ/ versus /e/; spellings of /eɪ/.
May; *will*; *going to*; present progressive as future; prepositions of time.	/əʊ/; 'dark' *l*; stress and rhythm.
Present perfect simple; present perfect progressive; non-progressive verbs; *since*; *for*; *used to*.	Letter *e* stressed and unstressed at the beginning of words.
Can for possibility; *may* and *will*; linking devices for writing.	/ʃ/ and /tʃ/; rising and falling intonation.
Present perfect and its contrast with simple past; *there has been*; *make* + object + adjective or infinitive; past progressive.	/θ/ and /ð/; decoding conversational expressions spoken at speed.
If-clauses in open conditions; *if* vs *when*; imperatives; present tense as future in subordinate clauses; *when* and *until*.	/ɪ/; pronunciations of the letter *a*.
General revision.	Fluency practice.

Unit 1

People

A Tell me about yourself

1 Listen to the conversations and practise the sentences.
Introduce yourself to some other students. Find out their names and where they come from.
Then introduce some students to each other.

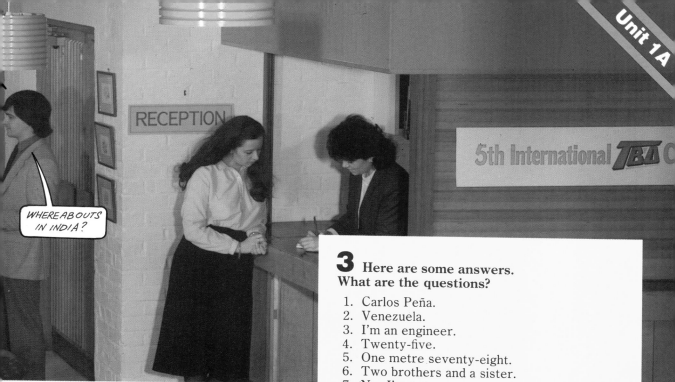

WHEREABOUTS IN INDIA?

RECEPTION

5th International TBA C

2 Match the questions and the answers.

1. What nationality are you?
2. Do you do any sport?
3. What kind of music do you like?
4. What kind of books do you read?
5. Are you shy?
6. Can you play the piano?
7. What do you like doing in your spare time?
8. Why are you learning English?
9. Where do you live?
10. Do you like watching football matches?
11. What does your father look like?
12. What's your mother like?
13. Have you got any brothers or sisters?
14. How do you feel about snakes?

a. Knitting and reading.
b. Mostly novels; sometimes history books.
c. Austrian.
d. She's very calm and cheerful.
e. In a small town near Vienna.
f. No, I'm fairly self-confident.
g. They don't interest me.
h. I prefer playing games to watching them.
i. Classical music.
j. He's tall and fair.
k. Yes, long-distance running.
l. I'd like to travel more, and I think it's a useful language.
m. Yes, two sisters.
n. Yes, but not very well.

3 Here are some answers. What are the questions?

1. Carlos Peña.
2. Venezuela.
3. I'm an engineer.
4. Twenty-five.
5. One metre seventy-eight.
6. Two brothers and a sister.
7. No, I'm not.
8. In a small flat in Caracas.
9. I need to read it for my work.
10. No, but I can speak a little French.
11. I watch TV or I go out with friends.
12. No, I don't, but I like dancing.
13. About twice a week.

4 Write some more questions to ask people in the class. You can ask the teacher for help, like this:

'How do you say marié?' 'Married.'
'What's the English for Leichtathletik?' 'Athletics.'
'How do you pronounce "archaeology"?'
'How do you spell ....?'
'What does "hobby" mean?'
'Is this correct: "............."?'

5 Interview the teacher. Find out as much as possible about him/her.

6 Work in pairs. Interview your partner and find out as much as possible about him/her.

7 Work in groups of four. Tell the other two students about your partner from Exercise 6.

8 Study the Summary on page 134.

B Married with two children

1 Copy the table. Then listen to the descriptions of the five people and fill in the details. Here are some of the words and expressions you will hear.

> JOBS: nurse; secretary; policewoman; printer's reader; works with racehorses; part-time.
>
> BUILD: slim; heavily built.
>
> CLOTHES: shirt; blouse; sweater; T-shirt; trousers; jeans; skirt; ear-ring; olive green; striped; short-sleeved.

NAME	Keith	Sue	John	Alexandra	Jane
AGE					
MARRIED?					
CHILDREN?					
JOB					
HEIGHT					
HAIR					
BUILD					
CLOTHES					

2 Can you put the right names with the photos?

3 Now listen to the recording of the five people talking. Try to note down the answers to the following questions.

1. What hours does Keith work?
2. How often does he go to church?
3. How does Sue get to work?
4. What does she like doing?
5. How old is John's daughter?
6. Does John like gardening?
7. How much does he say he drinks?
8. Does Alexandra read history books?
9. What newspaper does she read?
10. How many hours a week does Jane work?
11. What does Jane not like reading?
12. Two of the five people are married to each other. Which two?

Before you start, make sure you understand these words and expressions.

antiques   cycling   darning socks   decorating
history   historical novel   mending   philosophy
science fiction   thriller
Dick Francis (a popular thriller writer)

Newspapers: *The Express*   *The Sun*
The Times   *The Sunday Times*   *The Telegraph*

4 How do you feel about each of the five people? Do you find them interesting or not? Intelligent or not? Shy or self-confident? Do you like or dislike them? Which one would you most like to meet? Which one would you least like to meet?

5 Pronunciation. Listen to the recording. How many words do you hear in each sentence? What are they? (Contractions like *I'm* count as two words.)

6 Work in pairs. Look at your partner carefully for one minute. Then close your eyes (or turn your back) and say what he or she looks like, and what he or she is wearing. Useful structures: *He/she has got...*
He/she is wearing... Examples:

'He's got dark brown hair.'
'She's wearing a light green blouse and black trousers.'

7 *Is* or *has*?

1. She's 37.
2. What's he done?
3. It's late.
4. He's 1m 85 tall.
5. She's got blue eyes.
6. He's wearing a dark suit.
7. She's hungry.
8. He's cold.
9. She's gone to London.
10. He's married.
11. What colour's your new car?
12. She's tired.

8 Do you like or dislike these things? Write them in order of preference. Then see if anybody else in the class has put them in the same order.

maths   dancing   dogs   snakes   babies
cooking   shopping   chocolate

Now complete the table.

I very much like ....
....
....

I quite like ....
....
....

I don't mind ....
....
....

I don't much like ....
....
....

I can't stand ....
....
....

9 Study the Summary on page 134.

Other worlds

A There's a strange light in the sky

1 Look at the pictures and listen to the commentary. There are some differences. What are they?

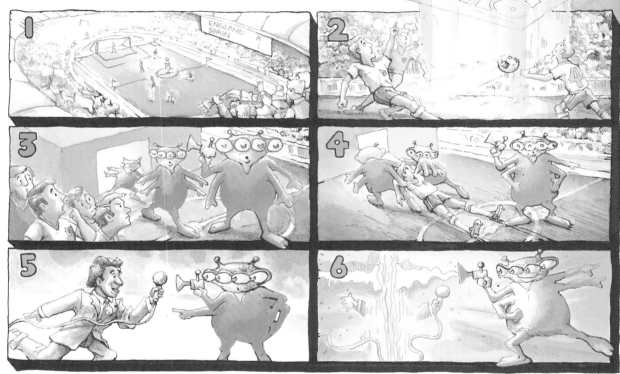

2 How well can you remember the commentary? Complete the commentator's sentences.

1. 'Everybody .... up.'
2. 'The light .... from a strange machine.'
3. 'A door .... in the top.'
4. 'A strange thing .... out.'
5. 'They .... green suits.'
6. 'Now they .... across the field.'
7. 'He .... him over to the spaceship.'
8. 'He .... him inside.'
9. 'I .... down to have a word with our visitors.'
10. 'It .... out a gun.'
11. 'It .... it at me.'

3 Pronunciation. Listen to each word, and say whether you think it comes in the commentary or not. Examples:

eat — No.
it — Yes.
green — I think so.
filled — I don't think so.

4 Pronunciation. Listen to the recording. Do you hear A or B?

A	B
eat	it
green	grin
sheep	ship
field	filled

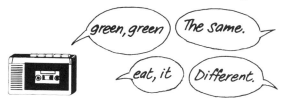

Listen to the recording and say whether the words are the same or different. Examples:

green, green — The same.

eat, it — Different.

Now say these words.

machine green field people believe dream in picture listen difference is coming thing him ship inside visitor think

5 You are the commentator. The strange creatures have taken you away with Evans in the spaceship. You still have your portable radio transmitter, and you go on sending messages to Earth to tell people what is happening.

Look at the pictures below, and work with other students to prepare a commentary. Make the commentary different from the pictures in four or five places.

Give your commentary, and see if the class can find the differences.

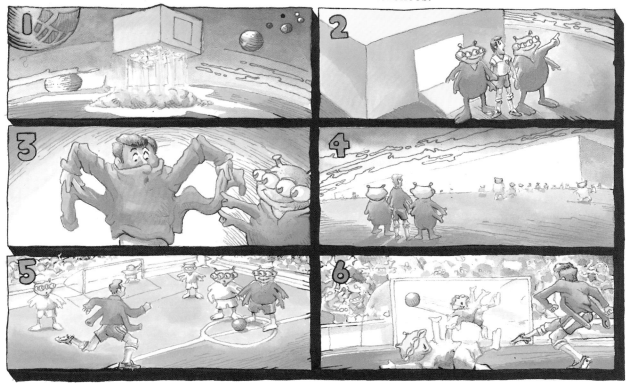

6 Study the Summary on page 135.

B What do you believe in?

1 What do you believe in?

a. Read the questions and choose your answers from the box. Write them down.
b. Work with another student. Guess how he or she has answered the questions, and write down your guesses. Then talk to your partner and find out if you were right.

1. Do you think that there may be intelligent life somewhere else in the universe?
2. Do you believe in 'flying saucers' (UFOs)?
3. Do you believe in ghosts (dead people who come back)?
4. Do you believe in reincarnation?
5. Do you believe in life after death?
6. Do you believe in a god?
7. Do you believe in telepathy?
8. Do you believe in horoscopes?
9. Do you think that some people can predict the future?
10. Do you think that we can learn important things from dreams?
11. Have you ever had experiences that you could not explain?

Possible answers:

'Yes, I do.'   'No, I don't.'
'Yes, I have.'   'No, I haven't.'
'Definitely (not).'   'Of course (not).'
'I'm not sure.'

---

2 Listen to the recording and fill in the table.
For each subject, write ✓ if the speaker believes in it, ✗ if he does not believe in it, and ? if he is not sure.

UFOs	
Life on other worlds	
Reincarnation	
Life after death	
Horoscopes	
Ghosts	

3 Pronunciation. Say these words.

believe   dream
in   think   thing   intelligent   predict

Now say these words and expressions.

thing   think   telepathy   death   I think there
that   the
there may be
I think that there may be
I think that there may be intelligent life in the universe.
I think that we can
I think that we can learn things from dreams.

12

4 Discussion. Work in groups of four or five. Talk about your answers to Exercise 1. Did you have more or fewer 'yes' answers than the others? Try to give reasons for some of your beliefs. Ask the teacher for help with vocabulary if necessary.

Useful expressions:
I agree with you.
I don't agree.
I think you're right.
Definitely.

Definitely not.
Yes and no.
Nonsense!
Rubbish!

Language Study

5 Grammar revision. Compare these pairs of sentences.

They're walking across the field.
They usually walk to work.

The light's coming from a strange machine.
Our light comes from the sun.

What are you drinking?
Do you ever drink beer?

What is the difference between *they are walking* and *they walk*; *it is coming* and *it comes*; *are you drinking* and *do you drink*?

6 Choose the correct verb forms.

1. He *is smoking* / *smokes* 20 cigarettes a day.
2. What *are you looking* / *do you look* at?
3. 'Excuse me. *Are you speaking* / *Do you speak* French?' 'No, but I *'m speaking* / *speak* a little Spanish.'
4. 'Come and have a drink.' 'I'm sorry, I can't just now. I *'m working* / *work.*'
5. 'Why *are you driving* / *do you drive* so fast?' 'Because we're late.'
6. I *'m going* / *go* dancing every Friday night.
7. '*Do you often travel* / '*Are you often travelling* abroad?' 'Four or five times a year.'
8. *Do you spell* / *Are you spelling* your name with one *n* or two?
9. 'What *are you thinking* / *do you think* about?' 'I'm not going to tell you.'
10. Water *is boiling* / *boils* at 100° Centigrade.
11. Can I turn off the TV? You *aren't watching* / *don't watch* it.

7 The same or different? You will hear ten pairs of words. If the two words in a pair are the same, write 'S'. If they are different, write 'D'.

8 Pronunciation. Can you hear a *th?*
Circle the words you hear.

1. mouth / mouse
2. thin / sin
3. thought / taught
4. thanks / tanks
5. there / dare
6. bathe / bays
7. they / day

9 Test other students. Say one of the words from Exercise 8. The other students have to say *Yes* if they hear a *th*.

10 Study the Summary on page 135–136.

XIII

LA MORT

The past

A A true story

1 Listen to the recording without looking at the text, and see how much of the story you can understand.

2 Read the text and fill in the gaps with words from the boxes.

ESCAPE FROM THE JUNGLE
(This is a true story.)

On Christmas Eve 1971 Juliana Koepke, a seventeen-year-old German girl, ... Lima by air with her mother. They .... on their way to Pucallpa, another town in Peru, to spend Christmas with Juliana's father. Forty-five minutes later the plane .... up in a storm, and Juliana .... 3,000 metres, strapped in her seat. She was not killed when the seat .... the ground (perhaps because trees broke her fall), but she .... all night unconscious.

The next morning Juliana .... for pieces of the plane, and .... for her mother. Nobody answered, and she .... nothing except a small plastic bag of sweets.

Juliana's collar bone was broken, one knee was badly hurt and she had deep cuts on her arms and legs. She had no shoes; her glasses were broken (so she could not .... snakes or spiders, for example); and she was wearing only a very short dress, which was badly torn. But she decided to try to .... out of the jungle, because she .... that if she stayed there she would die.

So Juliana .... to walk. She did not .... anything to eat, and as the days went by she got weaker and weaker. She was also in bad trouble from insect bites. She .... helicopters, but could not see them above the trees, and of course they could not see her. One day she .... three seats and .... that they had dead bodies in them, but she did not recognise the people.

After four days she .... to a river. She saw caimans and piranhas, but she .... that they do not usually attack people. So Juliana walked and .... down the river for another five days. At last she .... to a hut. Nobody was there, but the next afternoon, four men arrived. They .... her to a doctor in the next village.

Juliana .... afterwards that there were at least three other people who were not killed in the crash. But she was the only one who .... out of the jungle. It took her ten days.

Put the correct forms of these verbs into the gaps marked ⬚.

be	break	call	fall
find	hit	leave	lie	look

Put the correct forms of these verbs into the gaps marked ⬚.

find	find	get	hear
know	see	see	start

Put the correct forms of these verbs into the gaps marked ⬚.

come	come	get
know	learn	swim	take

---

sweets

snake

spider

piranha

caiman

hut

helicopter

5 Prepare five questions about the text. Example:

'When did Juliana leave Lima?'

When you are ready, work with another student. Close your book. Ask your questions, and answer your partner's.
If you have problems understanding each other, use these sentences to help you.

'Sorry, could you say that again?'
'I'm sorry, I don't understand.'
'What do you mean?'

If you can't answer a question, say:

'Sorry, I don't know.'
'I'm afraid I can't remember.'

6 Pronunciation. Copy these words. Then listen to the recording and circle the words you hear.

1. works / worked
2. rains / rained
3. starting / started
4. There's / There was
5. smells / smelt
6. stops / stopped
7. There's / There was
8. try / tried
9. puts / put
10. using / uses

3 Can you remember what you read? Close your book, listen to the recording, and write 'S' ('the same') or 'D' ('different') for each sentence.

4 Put in the correct forms.

1. How did Juliana *leave* / *left* Lima?
2. She *leave* / *left* by air.
3. How far did Juliana *fall* / *fell*?
4. She *fall* / *fell* 3,000 metres.
5. What did Juliana *look* / *looked* for?
6. She *look* / *looked* for pieces of the plane.

7 Work in groups of five or six. Tell other students about a bad day in your life.

8 Study the Summary on page 136.

B Did you have a good day?

1 Listen to the conversation with your book closed. Who did Lorna talk to during the day?

GEORGE: Hello, darling. Did you have a good day?
LORNA: Not bad. The usual sort of thing. Meetings, phone calls, letters. You know.
GEORGE: Did you see anybody interesting?
LORNA: Well, Chris came into the office this morning. We had a long talk.
GEORGE: Oh, yes? What about?
LORNA: Oh, this and that. Things. You know.
GEORGE: I see.
LORNA: And then Janet turned up. As usual. Just when I was trying to finish some work.
GEORGE: So what did you do?
LORNA: Had lunch with her.
GEORGE: Where did you go? Somewhere nice?
LORNA: No. Just the pub round the corner. A pie and a pint, you know. Then in the afternoon there was a budget meeting. It went on for hours.
GEORGE: Sounds like a boring day. Did anything interesting happen?
LORNA: Don't think so, not really. Can't remember. Oh, yes, one thing. Something rather strange.
GEORGE: What?
LORNA: Well, it was this evening. I was getting ready to come home. And the phone rang. So I picked it up. And there was this man.
GEORGE: Who?
LORNA: Well, I don't know. He wouldn't say who he was. But he asked me to have lunch with him tomorrow.
GEORGE: What?
LORNA: Yes. He said he wanted to talk to me. About something very important.
GEORGE: So what did you say?
LORNA: Well, I said yes, of course. How was your day?

2 Look at this sentence.

Had lunch with her.

Lorna leaves out the pronoun *I*. Can you find any more sentences where Lorna leaves out words?

3 Now listen again to George's side of the conversation with your book closed. Can you remember the beginnings of Lorna's answers?

4 Pronunciation: the letter *a*. Can you pronounce these words?

1. bad   had   happen   rang   man   (/æ/)
2. darling   afternoon   rather   ask   glass   (/ɑː/)
3. came   strange   day   say   train (/eɪ/)
4. call   talk   saw   (/ɔː/)

Put these words in group 1, 2, 3 or 4.

wait   hate   hard   glass   start   law   car
bath   late   ball   black   make   paid   arm
rain   fall   hat   part   happy   half   past
awful   may   all   stand   walk

Special pronunciations:

what   wasn't   want   watch   swan   (/ɒ/)
many   any   again   says   said   ate   (/e/)
about   America   England   umbrella   (/ə/)

5 Grammar: simple past and past progressive. Study the examples.

> *Just when I* **was trying** *to finish some work*
> ——————————————————————
> Janet
> **turned** *up.*
>
> *I* **was getting** *ready to come home*
> ——————————————————————
> *and the*
> *phone* **rang**.

Now put the correct verb forms into the sentences.

1. Andrew .... when I was getting ready to go out. (*arrive*)
2. The phone rang while I .... a bath. (*have*)
3. I first met my wife when I .... in Berlin. (*study*)
4. When I looked out of the window, it .... (*rain*)
5. I stopped because the car .... a funny noise. (*make*)
6. Where were you going when I .... you yesterday? (*see*)
7. When I was cleaning the house, I .... some old love letters. (*find*)
8. The accident .... while we .... into Copenhagen. (*happen; drive*)
9. I .... all my money when I .... from Istanbul to Athens. (*lose; travel*)
10. When I .... her, she .... reading. (*see; sit*)
11. The lights all .... while we .... supper. (*go out; have*)
12. When I .... the train, I .... my ticket onto the railway line. (*get off; drop*)

6 Imagine that it is six o'clock in the evening. You have just arrived home after an interesting day. What did you do? Make up answers to the following questions (ask the teacher for help if necessary).

What is your job?
How did you spend the morning?
Where did you have lunch? What did you have?
How did you spend the afternoon?
What places did you go to? Why?
You saw somebody interesting during the day. Who? When did you meet? ('*When I was . . . ing.*') What did you talk about? What did you do together?
Something interesting or strange happened during the day. What? When did it happen? ('*When I was . . . ing.*')

7 Work in pairs. You and your partner are members of the same family, or husband and wife, or flatmates or roommates in college. Talk about how you both spent your day (using the ideas from Exercise 6).
Useful expressions:

Did you have a good day?
Did you see anybody interesting?
What about?
You know.
I see.
as usual
So what did you do?
Where did you go?
What did you say?
What happened then?
Did anything interesting happen?
Not really.
(It) sounds like a boring/interesting day.

8 Work in groups. Tell the group what you did yesterday; or tell them about your last holiday; or about a journey that you made once; or about your earliest memory.

9 Study the Summary on page 137.

Comparisons

A Things are different

1 Look at the pictures. How many differences can you find between them?

Example: *'The fridge is bigger in picture B.'*

A   B

2 Revision. *-er* or *more*?

Examples: tall ...... *taller*

         important *more important*

old   interesting   beautiful   long   short
difficult   small   easy   cheap   expensive

-est or *most*?

Examples: tall ...... *tallest*

         important *most important*

fast   heavy   surprising   cheerful   boring
nice   young   light   intelligent   hard

3 Copy the table. Then listen and fill in the gaps.

	A	B	C	D	E	F
Number of wheels	4					
How many people does it carry?						1
Top speed (in kph)						
Weight (in kilos)						
Price (in pounds)						

18

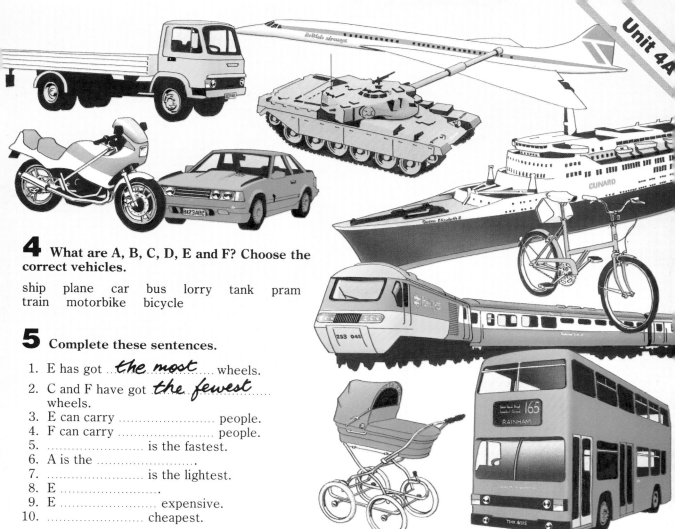

4 What are A, B, C, D, E and F? Choose the correct vehicles.

ship plane car bus lorry tank pram
train motorbike bicycle

5 Complete these sentences.

1. E has got *the most* wheels.
2. C and F have got *the fewest* wheels.
3. E can carry .... people.
4. F can carry .... people.
5. .... is the fastest.
6. A is the ....
7. .... is the lightest.
8. E ....
9. E .... expensive.
10. .... cheapest.

6 Listen to the recording. How many words do you hear in each sentence? (Contractions like *she's* count as two words.)

7 Look at the table and make some sentences (some true, some false). Ask other students if they are true or false. Use these structures:

...... has got more wheels than ......
...... hasn't got as many wheels as ......
...... can carry (far) more people than ......
...... can't carry (nearly) as many people
    as ......
...... is (much) faster/heavier than ......
...... costs (much) more than ......
...... doesn't cost (nearly) as much as ......
    (OR: ...... costs much less than ......)
...... has got the most/fewest ......
...... can carry the most/fewest ......
...... is the fastest/slowest/heaviest/etc.

8 Choose one of these groups of things. Ask other students which of the things in the group they would most like to have, and why. Ask as many people as possible, and write down the answers.

1. a dog   a cat   a horse   a bird
2. a Rolls Royce   a Citroen 2CV   a motorbike   a bicycle
3. a piano   a guitar   a violin   a trumpet
4. a holiday in the mountains / by the sea / in London / in San Francisco
5. a flat   a cottage   a big house
6. more money   more intelligence more free time   more friends

9 Tell the class what you found out in Exercise 8. Example:

'I asked about Group 1. Most people would prefer a bird, because it doesn't eat as much as the others.'
(OR: *'... it eats less than the others.'*)

B People are different

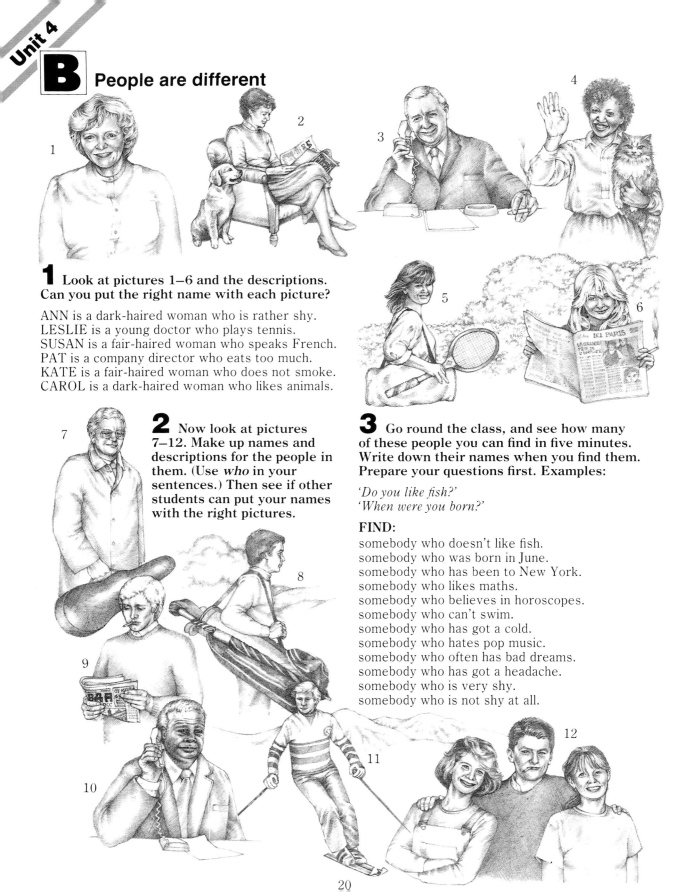

1 Look at pictures 1–6 and the descriptions. Can you put the right name with each picture?

ANN is a dark-haired woman who is rather shy.
LESLIE is a young doctor who plays tennis.
SUSAN is a fair-haired woman who speaks French.
PAT is a company director who eats too much.
KATE is a fair-haired woman who does not smoke.
CAROL is a dark-haired woman who likes animals.

2 Now look at pictures 7–12. Make up names and descriptions for the people in them. (Use *who* in your sentences.) Then see if other students can put your names with the right pictures.

3 Go round the class, and see how many of these people you can find in five minutes. Write down their names when you find them. Prepare your questions first. Examples:

'Do you like fish?'
'When were you born?'

FIND:
somebody who doesn't like fish.
somebody who was born in June.
somebody who has been to New York.
somebody who likes maths.
somebody who believes in horoscopes.
somebody who can't swim.
somebody who has got a cold.
somebody who hates pop music.
somebody who often has bad dreams.
somebody who has got a headache.
somebody who is very shy.
somebody who is not shy at all.

4 Listen to the recording, and decide whether the following sentences are true or false.

1. Keith is much taller than John.
2. Keith and John are both slim.
3. They both like gardening.
4. Keith's hair is darker than John's.
5. Keith has some sort of dressing in his hair.
6. John's face is thinner than Keith's.
7. Keith is wearing a black striped T-shirt.
8. John is wearing black shoes.
9. John is wearing black socks.

5 Pronunciation. Say these sentences. Pay attention to stress, rhythm and linking.

1. My **bro**ther and **I** are **very different**.
2. He's **not nearly as old** as **me**.
3. He's **much taller** than **me**.
4. His **in**terests are **different** from **mine**.
5. He **looks like** our father, but **I look like** our **mo**ther.
6. He **likes foot**ball, but **I don't**.
7. He enjoys **par**ties **much more** than **I do**.
8. He's interested in com**pu**ters, but **I'm** not.
9. My **sis**ter and **I** are **quite si**milar.
10. We **both have fair hair**, and we are **both left-hand**ed.
11. Her **eyes** are the **same colour** as **mine**.
12. We **both play** the piano.
13. She **sings bet**ter than **I do**.
14. We were **both born** in Sep**tem**ber.
15. She **likes trav**elling, but **I don't**.
16. **Both** of us **play ten**nis.
17. **Nei**ther of us can **swim**.
18. She is a **bit tall**er than **me**.
19. We are **both ra**ther **shy**, and we **both like li**ving a**lone**.

"Got any S shirts?"

6 A person with dark hair is *dark-haired*. Somebody who writes with his or her left hand is *left-handed*. What are the adjectives for these people?

1. a person with brown hair
2. somebody with blue eyes
3. a person who has broad shoulders
4. people who write with their right hands
5. a person with a thin face
6. somebody with long legs

Now say these in another way.

1. a blue-eyed girl
   'a girl with blue eyes'
2. a brown-haired man
   'a man . . .'
3. a left-handed child
   'a child who . . .'
4. a fat-faced person
   'somebody who has . . .'
5. a dark-eyed woman
   '. . .'
6. a long-sleeved pullover
   '. . . with . . .'

7 Work with a student that you don't know very well. Write down three ways in which you think you are different from your partner, and three ways in which you think you are similar. Then exchange your papers and discuss what you wrote. Were you right?

8 Now find out more about your partner. Try to find at least five things that you have in common, and at least five differences, and write them down. Use some of the language from Exercise 5; ask your teacher for words you don't know.
Useful expressions:

'Do you mind if I ask you a personal question?'
'No, that's all right.'

'How old are you?'
'I would rather not answer.'

Asking and offering

A **Have you got some stuff for cleaning windows?**

1 Vocabulary revision. Where do you buy these things?

meat bread vegetables sugar shoes
soap books clothes writing paper petrol
stamps aspirin films

Example:

'You buy sugar at a grocer's or at a supermarket.'

2 Look at the conversations and try to fill in some of the gaps. Then listen to the recording and write the complete conversations.

1. 'Good afternoon.'
   'Hello. .... a shampoo for dry hair.'
   'Large, medium or ....?'
   '..................... the small bottle?'
   '76p.'
   '..................... two bottles, please.'

2. '.....................?'
   'Yes, ...'

3. 'Can I help you?'
   '..................... I'm being served.'

4. '.....................?'
   '..................... a child's tricycle.'
   'Yes. .... the child?'

5. '..................... a pint of milk, please?'
   'Yes, of course. ....
   ....?'
   'No, ..., thanks.
   ....?'
   '24p.'

6. 'Hello, Sid. .... any flashbulbs?'
   'I'm afraid not, Fred. ....
   some in next week. Can you look in on Monday?'
   '..................... be away on Monday, but I'll call in on Tuesday.'
   'OK. ....'
   'Bye, Sid.'

7. '..................... a dishwasher.'
   '............. .... make?'
   '..................... Kleenwash XJ126?'
   'Yes, we have. It's a very good machine.'
   '..................... guarantee?'
   'Five years, madam.'
   '..................... deliver?'
   'Yes, we do, sir. Up to 20 miles.'
   'How much is it?'
   '....................., plus VAT.'

3 Rhythm and stress. Say these expressions.

Good **after**noon.
I'm be**ing served**.
a **pint** of **milk**
a **child's tri**cycle
Yes, we have.
Yes, of **course**.
Here you are.
I'm a**fraid not**.
the **small bo**ttle
How much is the **small bo**ttle?
How much is it?
How old is the **child**?
It's a **very good** ma**chine**.

4 Dialogue practice. Work with a partner and practise one or more of the conversations from Exercise 2.

5 Here are some ways to ask for things when you don't know the word.

Useful words:

a thing	stuff	square
a machine	liquid	round
a tool	powder	
	material	

Useful structures:

a thing **with** a hole / **with** a handle

a machine **for making** holes
a tool **for cutting** wood
a thing **for putting** pieces of paper together

some material **for making** curtains
some liquid **for cleaning** windows
some powder **for washing** clothes
some stuff **for killing** insects

Example:
A: *Excuse me. I don't speak English very well. What do you call the round glass in a camera?*
B: *The lens.*
A: *The lens. OK. I need some material for cleaning the lens.*
B: *A lens cleaner. Yes, we have ...*

Now look at the pictures and ask for one of the things illustrated.

6 Dramatisation. Work in pairs or groups of three. Prepare and practise conversations in shops. Use some of the expressions from Exercises 2 and 5.

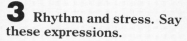

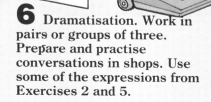

23

B I haven't got anything to wear

1 Read the conversation and then listen to the recording. How many differences can you find?

JAN: Hello, Kate. What's the matter?

KATE: Hello, Jan. Oh, dear. I'm going out with Tony tonight, and I haven't got anything to wear.

JAN: What about your blue dress? That's lovely

KATE: That old thing? No. It makes me look like a sack of potatoes.

JAN: Well, why don't you borrow something of mine?

KATE: Could I really?

JAN: Yes, of course. Would you like to?

KATE: Well, I'd love to. If you really don't mind.

JAN: What about that green silk thing?

KATE: Green silk?

JAN: Yes, you know. The dress I wore to Andy's birthday party.

KATE: Oh, yes. I remember.

JAN: You'd look great in that.

KATE: Oooh!

JAN: And I'll lend you my new shoes to go with it.

KATE: My feet are bigger than yours.

JAN: I don't think they are, Kate. Anyway, try the shoes and see. What about a jacket? Have you got one that will do?

KATE: Not really.

JAN: Well. have one of mine.

KATE: Oh, Jan. I feel bad, borrowing all your things.

JAN: That's all right. What are friends for? I'll borrow something of yours one of these days.

KATE: Well, thanks a million, Jan. I'd better get moving. Tony's coming in half an hour.

JAN: OK. Wait a second. I'll go and get the dress. Shall I iron it for you?

KATE: Oh, Jan, . . .

2 Match the questions and answers.

1. Can you lend me some stamps?
2. Excuse me. Have you got the time?
3. Can I borrow your pen?
4. Could you help me for a few minutes?
5. Have you got a light?
6. Shall I post these letters for you?
7. Could I borrow your bicycle for half an hour?
8. Have you got change for £1?
9. Could I use your phone?
10. Would you like to play tennis this evening?
11. Excuse me. Can you tell me the way to the station?
12. I'll give you a hand with the cooking, shall I?

a. Sorry, I don't smoke.
b. I think so. How many do you need?
c. Sorry, I'm afraid I'm using it.
d. Sorry, I'm not free. My son's coming round.
e. Just after half past three.
f. Perhaps – I'll have a look. Yes, here you are.
g. OK. Can you put it back on my desk when you've finished with it?
h. That's very kind of you. Could you do the potatoes?
i. Well, I'm in a bit of a hurry.
j. Of course. It's over there on the table.
k. Sorry, I'm a stranger here myself.
l. Yes, please, if you don't mind.

3 Pronunciation. Which words do you hear?

A	B		A	B
sale	sell		paper	pepper
late	let		pain	pen
gate	get		whale	well
main	men		wait	wet

Now pronounce some of the words yourself. Ask other students which words they think you are saying.

4 Pronunciation and spelling. Say these words.

1. Kate   change   table   strange   make
2. day   way   play
3. wait   chain   fail
4. station   pronunciation

Can you think of any more words to put into groups 1, 2, 3 and 4?

5 Grammar. Infinitive with or without *to*?

1. I haven't got anything *to eat / eat*.
2. Why don't you *to take / take* a holiday?
3. I would like *to go / go* out tonight.
4. 'That's the doorbell.' 'I'll *to go / go*.'
5. Can you *to lend / lend* me some money?
6. That dress makes her *to look / look* funny.
7. I hope *to see / see* you again soon.
8. Shall I *to carry / carry* that bag for you?
9. What time do you have *to start / start* work in the mornings?
10. It's nice *to see / see* you again.

6 Ask other students if you can borrow things from them. Use questions and answers from Exercise 2.

7 Write two or more notes to other students. In your notes, you must ask somebody for something, offer something to somebody, or offer to do something for somebody. Answer the notes that you get. Use words and expressions from Exercises 1 and 2.

Dear Anne,
Could I borrow your bike this evening? Yours, Patricia

Dear Pat,
Of course you can,
I'll give it to you
after the lesson.
Anne

Dear Tony,
Shall I drive you
to the airport on
Saturday?
Love,
Alice

Dear Alice,
Thank you very much.
That's very kind of you.
My plane's at 11.30.
Love,
T.

The future

A Their children will have blue eyes

1 How much do you know about genetics? See if you can complete the sentences correctly. When you have finished, ask the teacher for the answers.

1. If both parents have got blue eyes, their children:
   - will certainly have blue eyes.
   - will probably have blue eyes.
   - may have blue eyes.
2. If both parents have got brown eyes, their children:
   - will certainly have brown eyes.
   - will probably have brown eyes.
   - may have brown eyes.
3. If one parent has got blue eyes and one has got brown eyes, their children:
   - will certainly have blue eyes.
   - will probably have blue eyes.
   - may have blue eyes or brown eyes.
   - will probably have brown eyes.
   - will certainly have brown eyes.
4. If a man (but not his wife) is colour-blind, their daughters:
   - will be colour-blind.
   - may be colour-blind.
   - will probably not be colour-blind.
   - will almost certainly not be colour-blind.
5. If a man (but not his wife) is colour-blind, their sons:
   - will certainly be colour-blind.
   - may be colour-blind.
   - will probably not be colour-blind.
   - will certainly not be colour-blind.

2 Look at the picture. The couple are going to have a baby. What do you think it will be like? Make sentences beginning *It will ...* or *It may ...*

3 Pronunciation. Say these words and expressions.

know   so   go   hope   don't   won't
I know   I hope   I won't
I don't know   I hope so   I won't go

Now say these words and expressions.

will   I'll   you'll   he'll   she'll
I'll tell   I'll think   you'll be
she'll have   it'll rain
I'll tell you tomorrow   I'll think about it
You'll be sorry   She'll have to go soon
Do you think it'll rain tonight?

Carol works in a computer firm. She is rather shy, and often gets depressed. She is not very interested in sport, but she likes playing tennis. She is very musical, and can play several instruments.

Lee is a bus driver. He is a very sociable, outgoing person, optimistic and cheerful. He likes sport, especially ball games. He is interested in science, and he is studying maths at night school. He is not at all musical.

4 What will your children be like? (If you already have children, talk about your grandchildren. If you're not going to have children, talk about somebody else's children.) Use *will*, *won't*, *may*. *I (don't) think*, *I hope*. Examples:

'I hope my children will be good-looking.'
'My children may be musical.'
'I don't think my children will be tall.'
'My children certainly won't speak English.'

5 What sort of world will your great-grandchildren live in? Make some sentences.

6 The difference between *will* and *is going to*. Compare:

She **is going to** have a baby.
The baby **will** have blue eyes, and it **will** probably have fair hair.
She hopes it **will** be a girl.

Now study this rule. Use a dictionary to help you if necessary.

– We use *am/are/is going to* when we can already see the future in the present – when future actions are already planned, or are beginning to happen.
– We use *will* when we predict future actions by thinking, hoping, or calculating.

7 Look at the pictures and say what is going to happen.

8 *Will* or *going to*?

1. Look out! *We'll / We're going to* crash!
2. I hope one day *I'll / I'm going to* have more free time.
3. *Mary'll / Mary's going to* marry an old friend of mine in August.
4. I can't talk to you now. *We'll just / We're just going to* have lunch.
5. Perhaps in a few hundred years everybody *will / is going to* have an easy life.
6. 'What are your plans for this evening?'
   'I'll / I'm going to stay at home and watch TV.'
7. 'John's starting university in October.'
   'Oh, yes? *What will he / What's he going to* study?'
8. If you and your husband both have green eyes, your children *will probably / are probably going to* have green eyes too.

9 What are your plans for this evening / tomorrow / the weekend? Examples:

'This evening I'm going to stay in and wash my hair.'
'We're going to spend the weekend in the mountains.'

27

B How about Thursday?

1

Here are the beginnings and ends of three conversations. Which beginning goes with which end?

A

'Parkhurst 7298.'

'Hello. Paul?'

'Hello. Who's that?'

'This is Audrey. I wondered if you were free .... Tuesday.'

'It depends. What time?'

'............ the afternoon?'

'Yes, I could be. Why?'

'Well, my mother's coming down, and I'd like you to meet her. About half past four?'

B

'Hello, John. This is Angela. I'm trying to fix the Directors' meeting. Can you tell me what days you're free next week?'

'Well, let me see. Monday morning's OK. Tuesday. Not Wednesday, I'm going to Cardiff. Thursday afternoon. Friday's a bit difficult.'

'How about Thursday two fifteen?'

C

'Hello. I'd like to make an appointment to see Dr Gray.'

'Yes. What name is it, please?'

'Simon Graftey.'

'Yes. Three o'clock .... Monday, Mr Graftey?'

'Three o'clock's difficult. Could it be earlier?'

D

'Tuesday two fifteen. Let me look in my diary.'

'No, Thursday.'

'Oh, I'm sorry, I thought you said Tuesday. Thursday two fifteen. No, I'm sorry, I've got an appointment until three. Could we make it later? Say three fifteen?'

'Well, there's a lot to talk about. It'll take a couple of hours, at least.'

'Shall we say Monday morning, then?'

'Monday morning. All right. Nine o'clock?'

'Nine. I think that's all right. I'll ring you back and confirm.'

'All right. But ring .... five, could you?'

'I'll call you back .... about half an hour, Angela. All right?'

'Right you are. Bye, John.'

'Bye.'

E

'Two thirty?'

'No, I'm afraid I can't manage two thirty either. I'm seeing somebody .... two forty. Is two o'clock possible?'

'Yes, that's all right. Two o'clock .... Monday, then.'

'Thanks very much. Goodbye.'

'Goodbye.'

F

'That's difficult. You see, I'm playing tennis .... a quarter past. Then it'll take me a few minutes to shower and get changed.'

'What about later? Say, five?'

'Yes, OK. I'll come round .... five. Your place?'

'My place.'

'OK. See you then. Bye.'

'Bye.'

2

Can you put these prepositions in the right places in the conversations?

at	at	in	in	on	on
on	before	until			

3 Listen to the conversations. Then look at the text and see how these words and structures are used. Ask your teacher for explanations if necessary.

1. Present progressive tense with future meaning (e.g. *My mother's coming down*).
2. *How about . . . ?* and *Shall we . . . ?* in suggestions.
3. *I'd like to . . .*
4. *I'll . . .* in promises.

Write down ten more useful words, expressions or structures to learn. Can you find any other students who have chosen the same expressions as you?

4 How many stresses? Where are they? Listen to the recording to check your answers.

I wondered if you were free on Tuesday. (3)
In the afternoon?
I'd like you to meet her.
I'm trying to fix the Directors' meeting.
Can you tell me what days you're free . . .
Friday's a bit difficult.
I'd like to make an appointment . . .
There's a lot to talk about.
It'll take a couple of hours . . .
I'll call you back in about half an hour . . .
I'm playing tennis until a quarter past.

5 Practise one of the conversations with another student.

6 Fill in your diary for Saturday and Sunday. Put in at least eight of the following activities (and any others that you want to add), but leave yourself some free time.

wash your hair   write to your mother
play tennis   buy a sweater   see a film
have a drink with a friend   go to a party
clean the kitchen   mend some clothes
practise the guitar   study English grammar
make a cake   do your ironing   wash the car
go to church   go and see your sister
do some gardening

SATURDAY
9.00 Clean kitchen
12.00 shop. Buy sweater.
Lunch with Sally.
Afternoon Tennis
5.00 Guitar lesson

SUNDAY
Morning: Wash hair and mend clothes
12.30 Drink with Carl
Afternoon - Write to mother.
Study

HELLO, ANN. ARE YOU FREE ON SUNDAY?

IT DEPENDS. WHAT TIME?

ABOUT THREE O'CLOCK?

THAT'S DIFFICULT. I'M PLAYING TENNIS. WHAT ABOUT LATER?

7 'Telephone' another student. Try to arrange to do something together at the weekend.

Things that have happened

A Have you ever...?

1 Listen to the song. You will hear it twice. The second time, try to remember the words that have been left out.

2 Ask and answer questions beginning *Have you ever eaten / seen / climbed / met / been to / broken /*...? etc.
Example:

HAVE YOU EVER EATEN OCTOPUS?

NO, I NEVER HAVE.

YES. I EAT IT EVERY DAY.

NO, BUT I'VE EATEN SHARK.

YES, I ATE SOME LAST SUMMER.

YES, I'VE EATEN IT TWICE.

3 Match the words and the pictures. Then ask and answer questions beginning *Do you ever...?* or *When you were a child, did you ever...?* Examples:

'Do you ever go walking in the rain?'
'When you were a child, did you ever go camping?'

1. refuse to take medicine
2. stay up all night reading
3. dream of being someone else
4. take part in demonstrations
5. go out alone
6. want to be taller or shorter

30

4 What are the differences between *Have you ever...?*, *Do you ever...?* and *Did you ever...?*

5 Choose the correct tense (present, present perfect or past).

1. When you were a child, *have you ever run / did you ever run* away from home?
2. My brother *has had / had* a fight with his neighbour last week.
3. *Do you ever / Did you ever* travel by boat?
4. *Have you ever broken / Did you ever break* your ankle?
5. I *have often dreamt / often dreamt* of having a billion dollars.
6. During the last three years, I *have travelled / travelled* about 100,000 miles.
7. 'Do you know Canada?' 'No, *I've never been / I never went* there.'
8. I've got a very interesting job, and I *meet / met* lots of famous people.
9. I *haven't liked / didn't like* grammar at school, but I'm very interested in it now.
10. *I've spoken / I spoke* to the President several times.
11. *Have you ever / Did you ever* put an advertisement in a newspaper?
12. When we were small, Mother *has made / made* us delicious ice-cream every Sunday.

6 Listen to some people talking about past experiences. For each experience put a ✓ if they have had it, and a ✗ if they have not.

	1	2	3	4
eating snails				
going to America				
spending more than a day in hospital				
running a mile				

Now listen again. Try to pick out these words, and write down the verbs that go with them.

quite often   twice   very often
never   ever   recently   on one occasion
before now

7 In groups of three or four, make a list of ten or more questions that you can ask about someone's life, interests, work, etc. Examples:

'Where did you live when you were a child?'
'Can you talk about two happy times in your life?'
'Have you ever studied music?'

8 Find a person from another group. Ask the questions that you have prepared (and other questions, too, if you like). Note the answers.

9 Write some sentences (about eight), using some of the information from Exercise 8. Don't use the person's name in your sentences.

10 Pass your sentences to the teacher, who will read them to the class. The class has to guess who the sentences are about.

"Fifteen years we've commuted together on this train; fifteen years all we've ever said to each other has been 'Good Morning' – I'd just like you to know, I love you."

31

B Here is the news

1 Complete these sentences and write them out correctly. (You may need to put more than one word in a blank.) To get the information you need, look at the statistics and the background information on Fantasia, and listen to the news broadcast.

1. The population of Fantasia has *doubled / trebled / quadrupled* since 1900.
2. The population of San Fantastico *increased / decreased / has increased / has decreased* since 1900.
3. Fantasia used to be highly industrialised, but now has a mainly agricultural economy. True or false?
4. The Fantasians .... to have parliamentary elections every .... years. Since 1980, they *have / had / have had* parliamentary elections every .... years.
5. Mrs Rask *is / was / has been* President of Fantasia for .... years.
6. Fantasia has just .... a .... of Friendship and Protection with Outland.
7. Outland .... be a Fantasian colony. It *became / has become* independent in ....
8. .... of Outland and his wife have just arrived in Fantasia for a state visit.
9. President Rask and Mrs Martin *know / knew / have known* each other .... a long time.
10. They *first met / have first met* at the Olympic Games in 19.. , where Mrs Rask *won / has won* a silver medal for the high jump.
11. Dr Rask .... just .... from a trip abroad.
12. He has been visiting Third World countries for the last .... weeks in his capacity as President of 'Families ....'.
13. The percentage of homeless people in Fantasia has *risen / fallen* considerably .... 1900.
14. Unemployment figures .... *improved / worsened* since 1950.
15. The percentage of women in paid employment has *risen / fallen* .... 1950.
16. A fire .... burning .... three days in Grand South Station.
17. It .... raining steadily .... the last .... weeks in Fantasia, and the river Fant .... burst its banks.
18. The heavy rains have ruined some crops, and .... prices in San Fantastico .... going up steadily for the last .... days. The Minister for Consumer Affairs .... announced that price controls on vegetables and fruit will come into effect ....

FANTASIA: SOME STATISTICS			
ITEM	1900	1950	TODAY
Population	20m	35m	60m
Population of San Fantastico	1.2m	4.3m	3.6m
Average number of children per family	4.5	3.6	2
Working week (hours)	54	49	42
Paid holiday (weeks per year)	0	2	5
Size of army	500,000	200,000	50,000
Homeless	23%	17%	8%
Unemployment	20%	7%	17%
Women in paid employment	18%	23%	79%
Percentage of workforce in agriculture	84%	66%	19%
Contribution of agriculture to Gross National Product	78%	51%	8%
Contribution of industry to Gross National Product	11%	38%	83%
Foreign tourists per year	?	30,000	6m

FANTASIA AND OUTLAND: SOME BACKGROUND INFORMATION

Since the revolution in 1886, Fantasia has been a parliamentary democracy. There are two Houses of Parliament: elections to both used to be held every seven years, but since the Electoral Reform Act of 1980, elections have been held every four years. The president is elected separately by popular vote; the last presidential election was held three years ago. Mrs Kirsten Rask, the current president, is a distinguished physicist. She is also a former Olympic athlete who won a silver medal for the high jump in the 1960 Games.

Outland was formerly the Fantasian colony of South Wesk, but has been independent since the end of the War of Independence in 1954. Relations between the two countries have become more friendly since Mrs Rask's election, and Fantasia has just signed a 'Treaty of Friendship and Protection' with Outland. President Martin of Outland was at university with the Fantasian President's husband, Dr Erasmus Rask, and Mrs Martin and Mrs Rask have been friends since they met at the 1960 Olympics.

2 Look at the two pictures. What differences can you see? Examples:

'There used to be a church to the right of the bridge.'
'People's clothes have changed.'
'People didn't use to travel by car.'

VIEW FROM WESK SQUARE AROUND 1890

VIEW FROM WESK SQUARE 1985

3 Grammar revision. Can you answer these questions?

1. A man says, 'I've been in France for six years'. Is he in France when he says this?
2. A woman says, 'I was in Japan for three years'. Is she in Japan when she says this?
3. Somebody says, 'I've worked with Eric for 30 years, and I worked with Sally for 25 years'. Which one does he still work with?
4. Somebody says, 'I did seven years' French at school'. Is he or she still at school?
5. You are in America. Somebody asks, 'How long are you here for?' Does the person want to know when your visit started, or when it will end?
6. What does 'How long have you been here for?' mean?

4 Grammar. Choose the correct form.

1. I *am writing / have been writing / wrote* letters for the last two hours.
2. I *am going / go / have been going* out with some friends tonight.
3. 'How long *are you learning / have you been learning* English?' 'Since last summer.'
4. When I was a child, we *have been living / have lived / lived* in a house by a river.
5. I *have had / have* this watch since my 18th birthday.
6. 'How long *have you known / do you know* Jessica?' 'We *have been / were* at school together 40 years ago.'
7. I *am / have been* ill for three days now. I think I'd better call the doctor.

5 Pronunciation. These words all have the letter *e* in the first syllable. In some of the words, *e* is pronounced /e/; in others, it is pronounced /ɪ/. Can you divide the words into two groups, according to the pronunciation of *e*? What is the reason for the difference?

become depend
democracy demonstration
economy effect election
employment end every
held medal president
reform relations return
revolution secretary
separate seven vegetable

6 Work in groups. Prepare a short news item, with information about what has happened recently in your country, in the world, in your class, or in Fantasia.

Know before you go

A Going to Britain

1 Look through the text to find the answers to these questions.

1. How can you write *fifty pence* in another way?
2. Where can you usually get a good inexpensive meal?
3. Where can you ask about an inexpensive place to stay?
4. Is all medical care for foreigners free in Britain?
5. Which is cheaper, travelling by train or travelling by coach?

Getting around   Trains are fairly good in Britain. If you are under 24 or over 65, or if you are travelling with a family, ask about 'railcards' for cheaper fares on the train. There are also coaches (long-distance buses) between some towns and cities; these are cheaper than trains. In towns and cities, there are usually buses, and in London there is also an underground. But the underground is not easy to use, so you should learn about it before you use it.

Writing home   Stamps can only be bought in post offices; but nearly every village (or part of a town) has a post office. Often it is inside a small shop.

Money   There are one hundred pence (100p) in a pound (£1). People sometimes say 'p' instead of 'pence'; for example, 'eighty p'. Not all banks change foreign money, but you can usually find at least one bank in each town that will do so.

Eating out   Restaurants are often expensive, and you cannot be sure the food will be good. But Indian and Chinese restaurants usually serve good meals at lower prices. Pubs sometimes do good inexpensive food. Fast food shops – fish and chip shops, hamburger shops – are cheap, but the food is not always very good.

Where to stay   Hotels are very expensive in Britain. A cheaper solution is a 'bed and breakfast' in someone's home. Information centres or tourist offices can help you to find these. There are also youth hostels and campsites in many places.

Medical care   If you get ill or have an accident while you are in Britain, and you must be treated before you return home, you can get free medical care. Your country may have an agreement with Britain for other medical care, too; ask at the British embassy or consulate before you leave. You may need a special paper from your country's national health service. If your country does not have an agreement with Britain, you may want to take out health insurance for the journey.

2 Say these words after the teacher or the recording. Notice the difference in pronunciation between *sh* and *ch*.

1. should   shop   show
   British   wash   push
2. change   cheap   chip
   coach   teach   each

Now pronounce these words.

ship   shut   cheque   shower   cheers
switch   cash   fresh   watch   finish

3 Notice *can* in the text:

*...you **can** usually find at least one bank...*
*...tourist offices **can** help you to find these.*
*Stamps **can** only be bought in post offices; ...*
*...you **cannot** be sure the food will be good.*
*...you **can** get free medical care.*

Now answer these questions.

1. What are seven things you can do in an airport?
   Example: '*You can have a meal.*'
2. What are five things you can and can't do in your city/town/village/neighbourhood?
   Examples: '*You can go swimming. You can't go skiing.*'

4 Look back at the text and decide whether *will* or *may* goes in each blank.

1. Not all banks in small towns in Britain .... change foreign money for you.
2. If you stay in a hotel in Britain, it .... be expensive.
3. Information centres .... have information about 'bed and breakfast'.
4. If 'bed and breakfast' is too expensive, there .... be a youth hostel nearby.
5. You .... have the choice between a train and a coach for travel from one city to another.
6. You .... only find stamps in post offices.
7. If you break your leg while on holiday in Britain, you .... not have to pay the hospital for treating it.

5 Look for these words in the text and notice how each one is used.

for example   but   these   also   it   and   so   too

Now choose one of the subjects from the opposite page (*Money, Where to stay*, etc.) and write about your own country or another country you know about. Try to use some of the words from the list. Then exchange papers with one or more students to read what they have written.

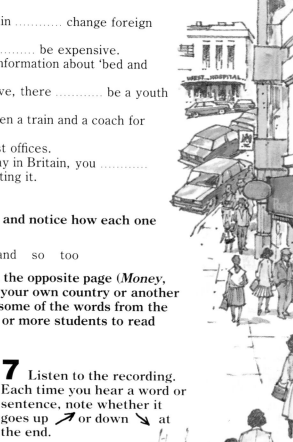

6 Listen.

1. Annie   Annie
2. Why?   Why?
3. in London   in London
4. July and August   July and August

Now listen again. Up ↗ or down ↘ ?

5. Annie   7. in London
6. Why?   8. July and August

7 Listen to the recording. Each time you hear a word or sentence, note whether it goes up ↗ or down ↘ at the end.

B Going to the USA

1 **What do you know about travelling in the USA? Try to answer these questions.**

1. A penny is worth one cent ($0.01, or 1¢). How much are these coins worth: a nickel, a dime, a quarter?
2. Can you usually find a bank in a small American town that will change foreign money?
3. In what places are you likely to find campsites in the US?
3. Is it easy to tour the United States by train?
5. What is the cheapest way of touring the States?

2 **Listen to the telephone conversation and write down the following information.**

1. the telephone numbers
2. the name of the person phoning
3. the time the plane will land
4. the airline and flight number

Now listen again and see if you can remember some of what was said.

3 **Work in threes. Imagine your wallet and passport have just been stolen in the airport in New York City. You were about to take a plane to Washington, and you still have your plane ticket and your traveller's cheques. Make some collect (reverse-charge) calls.**

1. To your friend Pat in Washington. Ask him/her to come and pick you up at the airport when you arrive. (Pat's phone number: (202) 664–3572)
2. To your cousin Chris, who lives in Newark, New Jersey, to ask him/her to phone and cancel your American Express and Diner's Club credit cards – you don't have the numbers of the cards, but your parents do. Chris can phone them if there is a problem. (Chris's number: (201) 435–2090)
3. To Mr/Ms Bennett, who is expecting you in Boston tomorrow. You will have to stay in Washington to go to your embassy and get a new passport. (The Bennetts' number: (617) 975–4303)

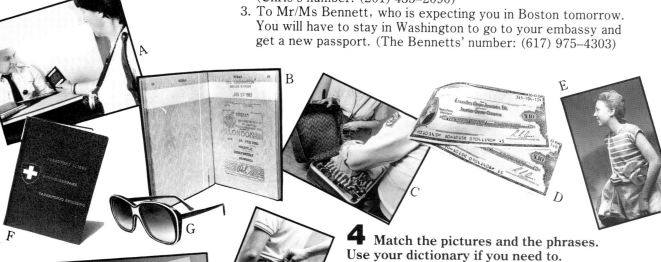

A B C D E F G H I

4 **Match the pictures and the phrases. Use your dictionary if you need to.**

1. a passport
2. light clothes
3. a pickpocket
4. customs
5. a visa
6. traveller's cheques
7. medical insurance
8. immigration control
9. sunglasses

5 Going to Miami. Make some sentences with *You'll have to* ... and *You should* ... for somebody who's going to Florida on holiday.

Examples: *'You should take sunglasses.'*
'You'll have to have a passport.'

> You should
> You'll have to

> have
> take
> watch out for
> go through
> buy

> a passport.
> light clothes.
> pickpockets.
> customs.
> a visa.

> traveller's cheques.
> medical insurance.
> immigration control.
> sunglasses.

NEW YORK, NEW YORK!
Spend two weeks in exciting New York City. Theatre, dance, opera, museums,...

WINNER TAKE ALL!
Come to Las Vegas and try your luck. When you're tired of winning at the casino, relax by the pool or go to watch a fabulous show...

WHITE WATER MAGIC
If you are a confirmed sportsman or sportswoman, spend an exciting two weeks with us canoeing in the beautiful Rocky Mountains...

DO IT YOURSELF
We provide the car or camping van, maps and advice, and you go your own way, discovering the America you want to discover.

ALOHA
You will never forget the warm welcome of Hawaii. Beautiful sunny beaches, friendly people, luscious tropical food...

FLOAT ALONG
Enjoy beautiful Texas scenery and wildlife while relaxing on a raft on the Rio Grande. Comfortable tent accommodation at night...

6 Which one of these holidays would you most like to win in a competition? Don't tell anyone else, but write down the reasons for your choice.

7 Try to find someone else in the class who has chosen the same holiday as you. Tell each other the reasons for your choices.

Then find people who have chosen another holiday. Tell them what you think they will have to do and should do.

Problems

A Emergency

1 Match the pictures and the sentences.

1. My baby has just eaten some aspirins.
2. There's a fire in my kitchen.
3. There's been an accident. A man is hurt. He's bleeding badly.
4. There's been a burglary.
5. Smoke is coming out of my neighbour's kitchen window.
6. Somebody has stolen my motorbike.

2 The same or different? You will hear nine pairs of words. If the two words are the same, write 'S'. If they are different, write 'D'.

3 Can you hear a *th*? Copy the list; then listen and circle the words you hear.

1. then / den
2. there / dare
3. think / sink
4. thing / sing
5. those / doze

4 Practise saying these after your teacher or the recording.

There's a   There's a fire
There's a fire in my kitchen.

There's been
There's been an accident.
There's been a burglary.

through   put you through
I'll put you through.

there   right there
We'll be right there.

think   I think
I think his leg is broken.

5 Look at the pictures and report the emergencies. Your teacher will help you.
Example: 1. *'There's a fire in the bedroom.'*

1

2

3

4

5

6 Phoning about an emergency. Here are some instructions from a British phone box.

SOS Emergency calls

Do not insert money; calls are free

Dial 999
Ask operator for **Fire** **Police** **Ambulance** **Coastguard**

01-654 8289
ON FOOTPATH
OUTSIDE 217 WICKHAM ROAD

'(Reproduced by permission of British Telecommunications.)

Now listen to the conversation and fill in the blanks.

OPERATOR: Emergency. .... service, ...?
FATHER: Ambulance.
OPERATOR: What .... are you ringing ....?
FATHER: ....
OPERATOR: Hold on. I'll .... you through.
OFFICER: .... Can I .... you?
FATHER: My .... has fallen off a ...., and I think his .... is broken.
OFFICER: Your .... and ...., please?
FATHER: Colin Jackson, ... Latton Close.
OFFICER: All right, ..., we'll be right there. .... cover your .... to keep him ...., but don't .... him.
FATHER: ....

7 Form groups of three. Choose emergencies from Exercises 1 and 5, or think of other emergencies. Invent and practise new conversations like the one in Exercise 6.

8 Think of an emergency in your life. Ask the teacher for any words you need to talk about it. Then tell the students around you what happened. Example:

'I wasn't very old, about 12. I was at home with my little brother. He pulled a very hot saucepan of soup on himself. I phoned..'

B You made me do it

1 Study and practise the dialogue. Your teacher will help you. Then work with a partner and make up a new dialogue, using some of the words and expressions you have learnt.

A: I'm sorry. I didn't mean to do it.
B: That's all right.
A: You see, I was thinking about something else. And I forgot what I was doing.
B: I see.
A: Actually, you made me do it.
B: I made you do it?
A: Yes. You coughed. You made me jump.
B: Yes. Well, it doesn't matter. We can get a new one.
A: I mean, it wasn't really my fault, was it?
B: No, it wasn't your fault.
A: I didn't do it on purpose.
B: No. Be careful!
A: It was an accident, you see.
B: Look out! Look out!!!
A: I mean, – **(CRASH!!!!!!!)**

2 Which picture? Listen to the sentences and write the answers. Example:

2. music

Then try to remember the sentence that goes with each picture.

a light switch | a brake | music | hard work

an accelerator | rain | chocolate | a kiss

3 Write four sentences of your own using *make*, like the ones in Exercise 2. Other students will try to guess what you have written about.

4 Read the story and put the pictures in order. Do not worry about the blanks.

A man had a row with his wife .... his breakfast was burnt. This made him leave home later than usual, ... he drove to work very fast. .... he was going round a corner, a dog ran across the road. The man stamped on the brakes, ... the car skidded (the road was in a very bad condition .... the City Council had not repaired it for a long time). The man lost control of his car .... crashed into a lorry .... was parked on a double yellow line.

Now put one of these words in each blank.

```
and    as    because    because    but
           so    which
```

5 Write the story that goes with these pictures. Try to use some of the words from the box in Exercise 4.

6 How many words do you hear? (Contractions like *there's* count as two words.)

7 Listen to the song. How much can you understand? (Words on page 156.)

If and when

A If you see a black cat, …

1 Match the beginnings and the ends of these sentences.

If you are travelling at 80kph in a car,
If your ancestors' language was Choctaw,
If the score is 40–15,
If today is your golden wedding anniversary,
If your great-grandparents all had blue eyes,
If you travel from England to Scotland,
In the 18th century, if someone saw a dodo,
If last year was a leap year (with 366 days),
If you can speak French,

next year won't be a leap year.
they were on the island of Mauritius.
you have been married for 50 years.
you can understand at least a bit of Italian.
you have blue eyes.
you can stop safely in 52m.
you do not go through immigration control.
you are probably playing tennis.
they lived in America.

2 Superstitions. Do you believe in luck? Complete the sentences with words and expressions from the box.

1. If .... a black cat, you'll have good luck.
2. If .... some wine, ... some salt over your left shoulder to keep bad luck away.
3. If the sky .... this evening, the weather is going to be fine tomorrow.
4. If your first visitor in the New Year .... dark hair, ... good luck all year.
5. You'll have bad luck if you: .... under a ladder, ... an umbrella in the house, or .... a hat on a bed. If you .... a mirror, you'll have seven years' ....
6. If the palm of your .... hand itches, you're going to .... some money.

bad luck	break	get	has	is red
left	open	see	throw	walk
you'll have	you see	you spill		

3 Do you know any other superstitions?

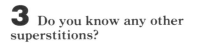

4 What will happen if ...?
Listen to the recording and
answer the questions.

5 *If* or *when*? Look at the difference.

When I go to bed tonight, I'll ...
   (I *will* go to bed.)
If I go to Scotland, I'll ...
   (I *may* go to Scotland.)

When you are on holiday, think of me.
   (You *will* be on holiday.)
If you are ever in London, come and see us.
   (You *may* be in London.)

1. .... I get rich, I'll travel round the world.
2. .... that's all you can say, I'm leaving.
3. .... I go to bed, I usually read for a few minutes.
4. .... you say that again, I'll hit you.
5. .... it rains this afternoon, we'll stay at home.
6. I'll close the curtains .... it gets dark.
7. .... I get older, I'll stop playing rugby.
8. Be patient; we can go home .... the game's finished.
9. Get on quickly .... the train stops.
10. .... you drive when you're drunk, you'll probably crash.

6 Listen to the recording
and do what the speaker tells
you.

7 Work in groups. Write
instructions like those in
Exercise 6 and give them to
another group.

8 Listen to the song once.
Then listen again and try to
remember the words that
have been left out.

43

B How to fill a kettle

1 Put a word or expression from the box into each blank. Then use the picture to help you put the sentences in order.

| as soon as then then |
| until when when |

.... it does this, it will turn the tap off. When you do this, the cat will run, turning the tap on.

.... you want to fill the kettle, hook its handle to the string and turn the small wheel .... the kettle is under the tap.

.... lower the fish to the right side of the cat's wheel.

.... turn the small wheel again to get the kettle back.

.... the kettle is full, move the fish to the left side of the wheel, and the cat will run the other way.

2 Look at the pictures and say what will happen. Example:

1. *'When / As soon as she opens the door, the light will go on.'*

3 Cooking tips. Put *when* or *until* in each blank.

1. Cook asparagus .... you can easily put a sharp knife through the middle of the stems.
2. If you need unsalted butter, pour boiling water over salted butter which has been cut into pieces, and then put it all into the fridge. .... the butter is hard, the salt will be left in the water.
3. .... you only need the yellow skin of a lemon, cut it with a potato peeler; this will cut it thinner than a knife.
4. If you are cooking whole onions, remember that they won't make you cry .... they lose their roots. So peel them from the top and cut the roots off last.
5. Serve vodka very cold. Keep it on ice .... the moment you pour it.
6. .... a melon is ready to eat, the end opposite the stem will be fairly soft.

(from *Supertips* by Moyra Bremner – adapted)

4 Work in groups. Make a list of three or more cooking tips to tell the class.

5 How do you tell when a cake or a loaf of bread is done? Listen, and complete the sentences.

1. Stick a needle in and see if...
2. Press it on the top and if it springs up again,...
3. Tap...
4. Cut...
5. Listen to it to see...
6. See if it's shrunk...

Now match the numbered sentences to the pictures.

6 Pronunciation. Pronounce these words.

1. handle cat back tap
2. way make cake
3. sharp hard class last
4. small all
5. want water what

You probably don't know these words. How do you think they are pronounced?

bark failing crack delayed
craft angle harm flash swab
tray wand sprain paw rate
stall nap vast balk shaft

7 In groups, invent a way of doing one of these things. Describe your invention to the other groups; you can draw pictures if you want.

1. Putting your shoes on without bending down
2. Opening and closing a window
3. Picking apples
4. Cleaning high windows
5. Washing socks

Now can you guess what these words mean?

needle spring tap bubble shrink

Revision and fluency practice

A A choice of activities

> Look at the exercises in this lesson. Try to decide which of them are most useful for you, and do three or more.

GRAMMAR REVISION

1 Choose the correct tense (present or present perfect).

1. How long *do you know / have you known* Mary?
2. *I live / I've lived* here for eight years.
3. *I'm going / I've been* home on Sunday.
4. *I have / I've had* this car since 1982.
5. Sorry I'm late. *Are you waiting / Have you been waiting* long?

2 Choose the correct tense (present perfect or simple past).

1. *Have you ever seen / Did you ever see* a boxing match?
2. *Have you ever been / Did you ever go* camping when you were a child?
3. Where *have you had / did you have* lunch yesterday?
4. Where's the telephone? *There's been / There was* an accident!
5. *I've never travelled / I never travelled* by air.
6. Can you help me? *I've lost / I lost* my watch.
7. *I've lost / I lost* my glasses the other day.
8. '*Have you had / 'Did you have* breakfast?' 'Not yet.'

3 Choose the correct tense (simple or progressive).

1. 'Could I speak to Linda?' 'I'm afraid *she puts / she's putting* the baby to bed. Could you ring back in about half an hour?'
2. I first met my wife when I *worked / was working* in Detroit.
3. How often *do you see / are you seeing* your parents?
4. My father *worked / was working* in Nigeria for a long time when he was younger.
5. *Do you know / Are you knowing* my friend Alex Carter?
6. 'Would you like a cigarette?' 'No, thanks, *I don't smoke / I'm not smoking.*'
7. 'What *do you do / are you doing*?' '*I try / 'I'm trying* to mend my bicycle. Would you like to help?'
8. 'What *do you do / are you doing*?' 'I'm a chemical engineer.'
9. 'I called at your house yesterday evening, but you weren't there. What *did you do / were you doing*?' 'I was at a party.'
10. 'What *did you do / were you doing* after the party?' 'I went straight home.'

LISTENING

4 Listen to the news broadcast and answer the questions.

1. The Distillers' Company are planning to 'axe' some jobs. How many – more than a hundred or less than a hundred? And how many plants are they going to close?
2. Three youths attacked a nineteen-year-old airman. Did he have to go to hospital? Was any money stolen, and if so, how much?
3. Two women tried to use a stolen credit card. What did they try to buy?   a) wine   b) spirits   c) cigarettes   d) a car.
   What colour car did they drive away in? Can you describe them at all?
4. People in Amport go to church for an unusual reason. What is it?
5. What has been stolen in Cassington, near Witney?   a) camping equipment   b) cooking equipment   c) a camera from a kitchen   d) camera attachments.
6. Which of these words do you hear in the weather forecast?
   *cool   cold   clouds   cloudy   snow
   showers   sunny intervals   wet   dry
   nineteen   ninety   north-westerly
   north-easterly   winds   strong   Tuesday*

5 Listen to the conversation. Every time you hear the name of a food, write 'F'; every time you hear the name of a drink, write 'D'.

Listen a second time. Write down an example of each of these: a hard thing, a soft thing, a liquid, a solid, a countable noun, an uncountable noun.

6 Pronunciation. Listen to the conversation. How many times do you hear *there's* and *there are* ? Make a note each time.

READING AND WRITING

7 Are you a peaceful person? Answer the questions as honestly as you can and then find out your total score. (But don't take the test too seriously!)

1. If you have ever been in a political demonstration, score 2.
2. If you have lost your temper during the last three days, score 3.
3. If you have ever driven at over 160kph, score 2.
4. If you have ever broken a cup, glass or plate on purpose, score 1.
5. If you have been in a fight in the last three years, score 3.
6. If you have seen a war film, gangster film, western or other violent film in the last month, score 1.
7. If you have ever been in love with two people at the same time, score 2.
8. If you ever have violent dreams, score 1.
9. If you have ever walked out of a job, score 2.
10. If you have ever watched a boxing-match, score 2.
11. If you like the town better than the country, score 1.

Your score:

0–7: You are a very peaceful person.
8–13: Average.
14–20: You are not at all peaceful!

8 Now make up your own questionnaire.
Suggestions: find out whether people are energetic, polite, cultured, generous, honest, shy, careful with money, fashion-conscious, interested in sport, interested in politics, sociable.

SPEAKING

9 'What's my job?' Choose a job and mime it (act it without speaking) to the other students. They will say what they think you are.

10 'What am I playing?' Choose a game or a musical instrument. Mime it to the other students. They will say what you are playing.

11 'What are we talking about?' Work in groups of three. Prepare a conversation in which somebody asks for something, or asks somebody else to do something. When you are ready, mime your conversation (without using the words) for the other students. They will try to find the words.

Are you a painter?

You're a conductor.

I think he's a policeman.

You're playing the harp.

Are you playing cricket?

Perhaps she's playing tennis.

12 Descriptions: revision. Read the conversation. Then work with a partner and make up a similar conversation about something that has been lost. Try to use the words and expressions in italics.

A: *I've lost* a briefcase.
B: Oh, yes? *What's it like?* Can you describe it?
A: It's brown, *with* a handle on top, and *it's got* a brass lock. It's about this big.
B: Anything inside it?
A: Yes. *There are* some books *with* my name *in*, and there's a pen *that* I bought yesterday. And a pint of milk.
B: *Where did you lose it?*
A: I think *I left it* on the number 14 bus.
B: Well, *I'll see what I can do...*

13 Question-box. Each student writes three questions on separate pieces of paper. One of the questions must begin *Have you ever...?*, and one must begin *Do you...?* The questions are folded up and put in a box. Students take turns to draw out questions and answer them.

B ## Knife-thrower's assistant wanted

WELL-KNOWN NORTHERN MANUFACTURER
requires
SALES MANAGER
for district between Liverpool and Carlisle.
Very good .....1...... and conditions.
Use of new company car.
.....2..... between 25 and 40.
Previous selling .....3..... essential.
.....4..... to: Managing Director, Domestic
Engineering Services Ltd, 417 North Way,
Whitehaven, Cumbria WN6 4DJ.

---

1 Read the advertisement and the two letters. Fill in the numbered gaps with words and expressions from the box. (You can use a dictionary, or ask your teacher about difficult words.)

advertised   age   apply   companies engineering   experience   faithfully look forward   salary   Sales Manager several   should like   worked   write

---

17 Grove Crescent
Greendale
Cumbria CU6 7LY

May 24, 1985

The Managing Director
Domestic Engineering Services Ltd
417 North Way
Whitehaven
Cumbria WN6 4DJ

Dear Sir

I ...5... to apply for the post of ...6... advertised in the Guardian of 22 May. I am 36 years old and have experience of selling in ...7... firms. I also have qualifications in ...8...

I look forward to hearing from you.

Yours faithfully

Roger Parsons

---

35 Allendale Road,
Carlisle
CA2 4SJ.

23 May, 1985

Dear Sir,

I wish to ....9.... for the job of Sales Manager ...10... in yesterday's Guardian. I have a Higher National Diploma in Business Studies, and have ...11... as a Sales Manager for two large ...12.... I am 29.

I ...13... to hearing from you.

Yours ...14...,

Andrew Jardine

---

2 Here are some sentences from four letters from Domestic Engineering Services Ltd to Mr Parsons and Mr Jardine. (The sentences are not in order; some of them come in more than one letter.) Can you write one of the letters?

Dear Mr ......
Yours sincerely
Please come for an interview on ...... at ...... a.m.
Thank you for your letter of ...... May.
Please confirm your acceptance as soon as possible.
Thank you for coming for an interview yesterday.
We regret that we are unable to offer you the post.
We are pleased to offer you the position of Sales Manager, starting on 1 August, at a salary of £12,500 a year.

3 Read the advertisements with a dictionary.

ROSTON TIMES

MANAGER FOR SMALL NEWSAGENTS

*Applicants must have experience
of running a small shop.
Good knowledge of accounting desirable.*
Aged 25–40.
Apply in writing to:
Personnel Manager
Chambers and Wren
Chambers House
High Street
Barbury BA6 10S.

Efficient
SHORTHAND TYPIST/SECRETARY
needed for small friendly company.
Apply to Office Manageress, Ann Harper Ltd,
6 Newport Road, Roston RS1 4JX.

FULL-TIME GARDENER
wanted for Roston General Hospital.
Experience essential.
Good wages and conditions.
Apply: The Administrator.

TEACHER REQUIRED
for private language school.
Teaching experience unnecessary.
Apply: The Director of Studies
Instant Languages Ltd
279 Canal Street, Roston.

CLEANER
required for our Roston office,
hours by arrangement. Apply The
Manager Coleman and Stokes 33
South Parade Roston RS1 5BQ.

Full-time
DRIVERS
required
Clean driving licence
Must be of smart appearance
Aged over 25.
Apply
CAPES TAXIS
17 Palace Road
Roston.

SECRETARY
(good Audio/Shorthand)

CABIN STAFF
Southern Airlines require cabin staff for
intercontinental flights. Applicants must be
between 20 and 33 years old, height 1m60 to
1m75, education to GCE standard, two
languages, must be able to swim. Apply to
Recruitment Officer, Southern Airlines,
Heathrow Airport West, HR3 7KK.

PART-TIME JOB
Circus has an unexpected vacancy for a
knife-thrower's assistant. Excellent pay. Apply in
writing to City Show Office, 13 Rose Lane, Roston.

SECRETARIES

Methodist Ch
Overseas Divi

SECRETA
ASSISTA

with good
qualifications to join
team dealing with
and introduction
prepared to have
responsibilities in
meeting people.
Further information
Path to Mary Jefers
London NW1 b.II
BN41).

PA/SECRE
(1000
Our client an established
Agency in W

---

4 Job interviews. Work in groups of about
six (three interviewers and three applicants)
1. Applicants write letters of application for
   one of the jobs advertised; interviewers
   prepare interviews.
2. Applicants are interviewed in turn.
3. Interviewers choose the best applicant and
   write letters to all three.

Where do you work? How long have you been there?
Why do you want to change your job? Where did
you go to school? Have you any experience of
selling? Can you speak any foreign languages?
Have you ever lived abroad? Have you ever been
dismissed from a job? What are your interests?
Are you married?

What's the salary? What are the hours?
Is there a canteen?

49

SUMMARIES

Unit 1: Lesson A

Grammar and structures

Introductions

Professor Andrews, this is Dr Baxter.
I'd like to introduce...
May I introduce myself?
Aren't you Henry Pollard?

'How do you do?' 'How do you do?'
I'm glad to meet you.
I've heard so much about you.
Nice to see you again.
I didn't catch your name.

Simple present tense

I work you work he/she/it works we work they work	do I work? do you work? does he/she/it work? do we work? do they work?

I do not (don't) work you do not (don't) work he/she/it does not (doesn't) work we do not (don't) work they do not (don't) work

Spelling:

he works   he stops   he starts   he likes
he wishes   he watches   he misses
he tries   he studies

Simple present tense: questions

    1   2   3
Where do you live?
      1   2   3
Where does your father live?
   (**NOT** ~~Where does live...~~)

Other structures

Where are you **from**?
What nationality **are** you?
What kind of books do you like?
Can you play **the** piano?
   (**NOT** ~~Can you play piano?~~)
What do you like **doing** in your spare time?

What does your father look **like**?
What is your mother **like**?

Asking for help in class

How do you say...?
What's the English for...?
How do you pronounce...?
How do you spell...?
What does...mean?
   (**NOT** ~~What means...?~~)
Is this correct: '...'?

Words and expressions to learn

kind /kaɪnd/
spare time /'speə 'taɪm/
football match /'fʊtbɔːl 'mætʃ/
classical music /'klæsɪkl 'mjuːzɪk/
answer /'ɑːnsə(r)/
work /wɜːk/
introduce /ɪntrə'djuːs/
interest /'ɪntrəst/
travel /'trævl/
find out (found, found)
  /'faɪnd 'aʊt (faʊnd)/
go out (went, gone out)
  /'gəʊ 'aʊt (went, gɒn)/
cheerful /'tʃɪəfl/
glad /glæd/
whereabouts /weərə'baʊts/
so much /'səʊ 'mʌtʃ/

Revision vocabulary: do you know these words?

nationality /næʃə'næləti/
sport /spɔːt/
novel /'nɒvl/
flat /flæt/
first name /'fɜːst 'neɪm/
Christian name /'krɪstʃən 'neɪm/
surname /'sɜːneɪm/
Mr /'mɪstə(r)/
Mrs /'mɪsɪz/
Miss /mɪs/
Ms /mɪz, məz/

Unit 1: Lesson B

Grammar and structures

Have got

I have got (I've got) you have got (you've got) he/she/it has got (he's/she's/it's got) we have got (we've got) they have got (they've got)

have I got? have you got? has he/she/it got? have we got? have they got?

I have not (haven't) got you have not (haven't) got he/she/it has not (hasn't) got we have not (haven't) got they have not (haven't) got

We use *have got* in informal English to talk about possession and similar ideas, especially in the present tense. It means the same as *have*.

I've got a small flat in the city centre.
Have you **got** today's newspaper?
My sister **hasn't got** any children.

Be and *have*

'How old are you?' '**I'm** thirty-five.'
  (**NOT** '~~I have thirty-five~~.')
I'm thirsty. **I'm** hungry. **I'm** hot. **I'm** cold.
What colour **is** your car?

Position of adverbs

Don't put an adverb between a verb and its object.

I **very much** like dancing.
  OR: I like dancing **very much.**
  (**NOT** ~~I like very much dancing~~.)
I **often** read thrillers.
  (**NOT** ~~I read often thrillers~~.)
I **never** get headaches.
  (**NOT** ~~I get never headaches~~.)
You speak English **very well.**
  (**NOT** ~~You speak very well English~~.)

Like ... ing

I **like** dancing.
Do you **like** cooking?

Articles

Jane is **a** secretary. (**NOT** ~~Jane is secreta~~
I like dogs. (**NOT** ~~I like the dogs~~.)

Words and expressions to learn

nurse /nɜːs/
secretary /ˈsekrətri/
policewoman /pəˈliːswʊmən/
T-shirt /ˈtiːʃɜːt/
ear-ring /ˈɪərɪŋ/
history /ˈhɪstəri/
newspaper /ˈnjuːspeɪpə(r)/
thriller /ˈθrɪlə(r)/
chocolate /ˈtʃɒklət/

wear (wore, worn)
/weə(r) (wɔː(r), wɔːn)/
mend /mend/
part-time /ˈpɑːt ˈtaɪm/
slim /slɪm/
striped /straɪpt/
least /liːst/
I don't mind /aɪ ˈdəʊnt ˈmaɪnd/

Revision vocabulary: do you know these words?

clothes /kləʊðz/
shirt /ʃɜːt/
blouse /blaʊz/
sweater /ˈswetə(r)/
trousers /ˈtraʊzəz/
jeans /dʒiːnz/
skirt /skɜːt/
age /eɪdʒ/
job /dʒɒb/
height /haɪt/
daughter /ˈdɔːtə(r)/
dog /dɒg/
baby /ˈbeɪbi/

meet (met, met) /miːt (met)/
dance /dɑːns/
cook /kʊk/
shop /ʃɒp/
married /ˈmærɪd/
intelligent /ɪnˈtelɪdʒənt/
interesting /ˈɪntrəstɪŋ/
light /laɪt/
dark /dɑːk/
I can't stand /aɪ ˈkɑːnt ˈstænd/

Unit 2: Lesson A

Grammar and structures

Present progressive tense

I am (I'm) working
you are (you're) working
he/she/it is (he's/she's/it's) working
we are (we're) working
they are (they're) working

am I working?
are you working?
is he/she/it working?
are we working?
are they working?

I am (I'm) not working
you are not (aren't) working
he/she/it is not (isn't) working
we are not (aren't) working
they are not (aren't) working

We use this tense to talk about things that are happening at the moment when we are speaking or writing.

I **am going** (I'm going) down to have a word with our visitors.
It **is coming** (It's coming) down very low.
Three strange things **are getting** out.

Present progressive questions

What **are** you **doing**?
   (1) (2) (3)
What **are** the President and his wife **doing**?
   (1)   (2)   (3)
   (**NOT** ~~What are doing...?~~)
Are you **enjoying** your meal?
 (1) (2)   (3)

Spelling of -ing forms

look   looking
open   opening

come   coming   } verbs ending in -e
take   taking

get   getting   } verbs ending in one consonant
stop   stopping } + one stressed vowel

lie   lying   } verbs ending in -ie
die   dying

Words and expressions to learn

light / laɪt/
sky /skaɪ/
machine /məˈʃiːn/
suit /suːt/
field /fiːld/
visitor /ˈvɪzɪtə(r)/
gun /gʌn/
strange /streɪndʒ/
round /raʊnd/

Revision vocabulary: do you know these words?

picture /ˈpɪktʃə(r)/
top /tɒp/
remember /rɪˈmembə(r)/
listen /ˈlɪsn/
square /skweə(r)/
across /əˈkrɒs/
inside /ɪnˈsaɪd/

Unit 2: Lesson B

Grammar and structures

The two present tenses

We use the *simple present tense* to talk about 'general time': permanent states and repeated actions.

Our light **comes** from the sun.
They usually **walk** to work.
Do you ever **drink** beer?

We use the *present progressive tense* to talk about things which are happening at or around the present moment.

The light **is coming** from a strange machine.
They **are walking** across the field.
What **are you drinking**?

Other structures

Do you **believe in** 'flying saucers'?
I **agree with** you.
I **don't agree with** you.
I **think** (**that**) you're right.

➡

135

Words and expressions to learn

death /deθ/
a god /ə 'gɒd/
the future /ðə 'fjuːtʃə(r)/
experience /ɪk'spɪərɪəns/
belief /bɪ'liːf/
reason /'riːzn/
expression /ɪk'spreʃn/
nonsense /'nɒnsəns/

rubbish /'rʌbɪʃ/
guess /ges/
choose (chose, chosen) /tʃuːz (tʃəʊz, 'tʃəʊzn)/
explain /ɪk'spleɪn/
definitely (not) /'defənətli (nɒt)/
yes and no /'jes ən 'nəʊ/

Revision vocabulary: do you know these words?

life /laɪf/
dream (dreamt, dreamt) /driːm (dremt)/
dead /ded/
sure /ʃɔː(r)/
intelligent /ɪn'telɪdʒənt/
somewhere else /'sʌmweər 'els/

Unit 3: Lesson A

Grammar and structures

Simple past tense

I walked
you walked
he/she/it walked
etc.

did I walk?
did you walk?
did he/she/it walk?
etc.

(**NOT** ~~did I walked?~~)

I did not (didn't) walk
you did not (didn't) walk
he/she/it did not (didn't) walk
etc.

(**NOT** ~~I did not walked~~)

I went
you went
he/she/it went
etc.

did I go?
did you go?
did he/she/it go?
etc.

(**NOT** ~~did you went?~~)

I did not (didn't) go
you did not (didn't) go
he/she/it did not (didn't) go
etc.

(**NOT** ~~you didn't went~~)

The past of *be*

I was
you were
he/she/it was
we were
they were

was I?
were you?
was he/she/it?
were we?
were they?

I was not (wasn't)
you were not (weren't)
he/she/it was not (wasn't)
we were not (weren't)
they were not (weren't)

Spelling of regular past tenses

work	work**ed**
listen	listen**ed**
cook	cook**ed**
play	play**ed**

live	live**d**	}
love	love**d**	} verbs ending in *-e*
hate	hate**d**	}

stop	stop**ped**	} verbs ending in one vowel
fit	fit**ted**	} + one consonant

marr**y**	marr**ied**	} verbs ending in consonant + *-y*
stud**y**	stud**ied**	}

Irregular verbs

Infinitive	Simple past	Past participle
come /kʌm/	came /keɪm/	come /kʌm/
fall /fɔːl/	fell /fel/	fallen /'fɔːlən/
find /faɪnd/	found /faʊnd/	found /faʊnd/
get /get/	got /gɒt/	got /gɒt/
go /gəʊ/	went /went/	gone /gɒn/
hear /hɪə(r)/	heard /hɜːd/	heard /hɜːd/
hit /hɪt/	hit /hɪt/	hit /hɪt/
hurt /hɜːt/	hurt /hɜːt/	hurt /hɜːt/
know /nəʊ/	knew /njuː/	known /nəʊn/
learn /lɜːn/	learnt /lɜːnt/	learnt /lɜːnt/
leave /liːv/	left /left/	left /left/
lie /laɪ/	lay /leɪ/	lain /leɪn/
see /siː/	saw /sɔː/	seen /siːn/
swim /swɪm/	swam /swæm/	swum /swʌm/

Words and expressions to learn

Christmas /'krɪsməs/
Christmas Eve /'krɪsməs 'iːv/
storm /stɔːm/
bag /bæg/
sweets /swiːts/
bone /bəʊn/
knee /niː/
cut /kʌt/
helicopter /'helɪkɒptə(r)/
call /kɔːl/
hit (hit, hit) /hɪt/

stay /steɪ/
recognise /'rekəgnaɪz/
deep /diːp/
above /ə'bʌv/
afterwards /'ɑːftəwədz/

Revision vocabulary: do you know these words?

town /taʊn/
seat /siːt/
piece /piːs/
plane /pleɪn/
plastic /'plæstɪk/
dress /dres/
river /'rɪvə(r)/
village /'vɪlɪdʒ/
glasses /'glɑːsɪz/
insect /'ɪnsekt/

spend (spent, spent) /spend (spent)/
kill /kɪl/
decide /dɪ'saɪd/
die /daɪ/
arrive /ə'raɪv/
wear (wore, worn) /weə(r) (wɔː(r), wɔːn)/
try /traɪ/
short /ʃɔːt/
dead /ded/
by air /baɪ 'eə(r)/

136

Unit 3: Lesson B

Grammar and structures

Past progressive tense

I was working you were working he/she/it was working we were working they were working	was I working? were you working? was he/she/it working? were we working? were they working?

I was not (wasn't) working
you were not (weren't) working
he/she/it was not (wasn't) working
we were not (weren't) working
they were not (weren't) working

Just when I **was trying** *to finish some work*
Janet **turned up.**

I **was getting** *ready to come home*
and the phone **rang.**

I **lost** all my money when I **was travelling from Istanbul to Athens.**
The phone rang while I **was having** a bath.

Ellipsis
(I) Had lunch with her.
(It) Sounds like a boring day.
(I) Can't remember.

Words and expressions to learn

darling /'dɑ:lɪŋ/
meeting /'mi:tɪŋ/
talk /tɔ:k/
phone call /'fəʊn 'kɔ:l/
memory /'meməri/
turn up /'tɜ:n 'ʌp/
go on (went, gone) /'gəʊ 'ɒn (went, gɒn)/
get ready /'get 'redi/
rather /'rɑ:ðə(r)/

together /tə'geðə(r)/
you know /'ju: 'nəʊ/
I see /'aɪ 'si:/
as usual /əz 'ju:ʒuəl/
round the corner /'raʊnd ðə 'kɔ:nə(r)/
sound like /'saʊnd 'laɪk/
not really /'nɒt 'rɪəli/
I can't remember /aɪ 'kɑ:nt rɪ'membə(r)/

Revision vocabulary: do you know these words?

letter /'letə(r)/
office /'ɒfɪs/
pub /pʌb/
pint /paɪnt/
journey /'dʒɜ:ni/
try /traɪ/
finish /'fɪnɪʃ/
ring (rang, rung) /rɪŋ (ræŋ, rʌŋ)/

Unit 4: Lesson A

Grammar and structures

Comparative and superlative adjectives

Short adjectives (one syllable) add -*er*, -*est*.
old older oldest

Short adjectives ending in -*e* add -*r*, -*st*.
late later latest

Short adjectives with one vowel and one consonant double the consonant.
big bigger biggest

Adjectives with two syllables ending in -*y* change *y* to *i* and add -*er*, -*est*.
happy happier happiest

Other adjectives with two or more syllables usually add *more*, *most*.
boring **more** boring **most** boring
expensive **more** expensive
most expensive

(See diagram, Practice Book page 18.)

Irregular comparatives and superlatives

good	better	best
bad	worse	worst
much	more	most
little	less	least

Comparatives and superlatives in sentences

A car is heavier **than** a bicycle.
It has got **more** wheels than a bicycle.
   (**NOT** ~~...more of wheels...~~)
A car is not **as** fast **as** a plane.
It has not got **as many** wheels as a plane.
A car does not cost **as much** as a plane.
   (**OR**: A car costs **less** than a plane.)
It is **not nearly** as heavy as a plane.
It costs **much/far** more than a bicycle.
A pram is **a bit** heavier than a bicycle.
A plane is **the heaviest** of the vehicles.

Words and expressions to learn

difference /'dɪfrəns/
wheel /wi:l/
vehicle /'vɪəkl/
ship /ʃɪp/
lorry /'lɒri/
pram /præm/
horse /hɔ:s/
bird /bɜ:d/
piano /pi'ænəʊ/
violin /vaɪə'lɪn/
trumpet /'trʌmpɪt/
cottage /'kɒtɪdʒ/
intelligence /ɪn'telɪdʒəns/
free time /'fri: 'taɪm/
top speed /'tɒp 'spi:d/

Revision vocabulary: do you know these words?

tall /tɔ:l/
short /ʃɔ:t/
long /lɒŋ/
old /əʊld/
young /jʌŋ/
small /smɔ:l/
important /ɪm'pɔ:tənt/
interesting /'ɪntrəstɪŋ/
beautiful /'bju:tɪfl/
difficult /'dɪfɪkʊlt/

Unit 4: Lesson B

Grammar and structures

The same
Her eyes are **the same** colour **as** mine.

Both
ONE-WORD VERBS
We **both speak** Chinese.
My sister and I **both like** music.

TWO-WORD VERBS
We **were both born** in September.
They **have both studied** in the USA.
Anne and Peter **can both sing** very well.

AM/ARE/IS/WAS/WERE
We **are both** fair-haired.
The two children **were both** very hungry.

Both/neither of us
Both of us like dancing.
Neither of us can swim.

Relative pronouns: *who*
Ann is a dark-haired woman **who** is rather shy.
Find somebody **who** speaks Chinese.

Compound adjectives
a **blue-eyed** girl
a **brown-haired** man
a **left-handed** child
a **long-sleeved** pullover

Do
She sings better than I **do**.
He likes golf, but I **don't**.

Like + -ing
I like ski**ing**.
Do you like danc**ing**?

Words and expressions to learn

fish /fɪʃ/
maths /mæθs/
company /'kʌmpəni/
director /də'rektə(r)/
pop music /'pɒp 'mjuːzɪk/
interest /'ɪntrəst/
party /'paːti/
computer /kəm'pjuːtə(r)/

hate /heɪt/
dark-haired /'daːk 'heəd/
fair-haired /'feə 'heəd/
similar /'sɪmələ(r)/
left-handed /'left 'hændɪd/
right-handed /'raɪt 'hændɪd/
broad-shouldered /'brɔːd 'ʃəʊldəd/
neither /'naɪðə(r)/
quite /kwaɪt/
I would rather not answer.
  /aɪ wʊd 'raːðə nɒt 'aːnsə/

Revision vocabulary: do you know these words?

a cold /ə 'kəʊld/
a headache /ə 'hedeɪk/
dream /driːm/
swim (swam, swum)
  /swɪm (swæm, swʌm)/
enjoy /ɪn'dʒɔɪ/
look like /'lʊk 'laɪk/
rather /'raːðə(r)/
shy /ʃaɪ/
alone /ə'ləʊn/
not...at all /'nɒt ət 'ɔːl/
Do you mind if...? /dju: 'maɪnd ɪf/
That's all right. /'ðæts 'ɔːl 'raɪt/

Unit 5: Lesson A

Grammar and structures

You buy meat **at** a butcher's.

a thing **with** a hole / **with** a handle
a thing / some stuff **for...ing**

Words and expressions to learn

soap /səʊp/
stamp /stæmp/
film (for a camera) /fɪlm/
tool /tuːl/
stuff /stʌf/
liquid /'lɪkwɪd/
powder /'paʊdə(r)/
material /mə'tɪərɪʊl/
hole /həʊl/
wood /wʊd/
guarantee /gærən'tiː/
make /meɪk/
cut (cut, cut) /kʌt/

deliver /dɪ'lɪvə(r)/
round /raʊnd/
Can I look round? /'kæn aɪ lʊk 'raʊnd/
I'm being served. /aɪm 'biːɪŋ 'sɜːvd/
I'm looking for... /aɪm 'lʊkɪŋ fə(r)/
That's all. /'ðæts 'ɔːl/
I'm afraid not. /aɪm ə'freɪd 'nɒt/
Anything else? /'eniθɪŋ 'els/

Unit 5: Lesson B

Grammar and structures

Infinitive with and without *to*
Can you **tell** me the way to...?
  (**NOT** Can you to tell me...?)
Could I **borrow** your bicycle?
  (**NOT** Could I to borrow...?)
Shall I **help** you?
  (**NOT** Shall I to help you?)
I'll **go** and get it.
  (**NOT** I'll to go...)

I would like **to go** out tonight.
  (**NOT** I would like go...)
I hope **to see** you again soon.
  (**NOT** I hope see you...)
It's nice **to see** you again.
  (**NOT** It's nice see you again.)

'Why don't you borrow something of mine?
  Would you like **to**?' 'Yes, I'd love **to**.'

Suggestions
What about your blue dress?
Why don't you borrow something of mine?

Words and expressions to learn

silk /sɪlk/
birthday party /'bɜːθdeɪ 'paːti/
change /tʃeɪndʒ/
iron (clothes) /'aɪən/
come round (to visit) (came, come) /'kʌm 'raʊnd (keɪm, kʌm)/
have a look /'hæv ə 'lʊk/
give somebody a hand (gave, given) /'gɪv 'sʌmbədi ə 'hænd (geɪv, 'gɪvn)/
put something back (put, put) /'pʊt 'sʌmθɪŋ 'bæk/
wait a second /'weɪt ə 'sekənd/
one of these days /'wʌn əv 'ðiːz 'deɪz/
Have you got the time? /'hæv juː 'gɒt ðə 'taɪm/
in a hurry /ɪn ə 'hʌri/
That's very kind of you. /ðæts 'veri 'kaɪnd əv 'juː/
I'm a stranger here myself. /aɪm ə 'streɪndʒə 'hɪə maɪ'self/

Unit 6: Lesson A

Grammar and structures

Will and is going to

We use *am/are/is going to* when we can already see the future in the present – when future actions are already planned, or are beginning to happen.

We're **going to** buy a new car.
She **is going to** have a baby.
It's **going to** rain.

We use *will* when we predict future actions by thinking, hoping or calculating.

If both parents have blue eyes, their children **will** have blue eyes.
I hope Ann **will** like these flowers.
We'll arrive in Edinburgh at about six o'clock.

May (= 'will perhaps')

If both parents are tall, their children **may** be tall too.
I **may** go to London tomorrow – I'm not sure.
(NOT I may to go...)
Mary **may** come and see us next week.
(NOT Mary mays...)

Words and expressions to learn

grandchild /'græntʃaɪld/
ball games /'bɔːl 'geɪmz/
science /'saɪəns/
firm /fɜːm/
(musical) instrument /'ɪnstrəmənt/
colour-blind /'kʌləblaɪnd/
sociable /'səʊʃəbl/
outgoing /'aʊtgəʊɪŋ/
optimistic /ɒptɪ'mɪstɪk/
musical /'mjuːzɪkl/
may /meɪ/
several /'sevrʊl/

Revision vocabulary: do you know these words?

parents /'peərənts/
daughter /'dɔːtə(r)/
son /sʌn/
couple /'kʌpl/
baby /'beɪbi/
computer /kəm'pjuːtə(r)/
bus driver /'bʌs 'draɪvə(r)/
sport /spɔːt/
maths /mæθs/
cheerful /'tʃɪəfʊl/
shy /ʃaɪ/
depressed /dɪ'prest/
certainly /'sɜːtənli/
probably /'prɒbəbli/
what...like? /'wɒt 'laɪk/
the future /ðə 'fjuːtʃə(r)/

Unit 6: Lesson B

Grammar and structures

Present progressive with future meaning

(Used to talk about future actions which are already planned or arranged, especially when we give the time or date.)

My mother's coming down on Thursday.
(NOT My mother comes down on Thursday.)
I'm going to Cardiff on Wednesday.
(NOT I go to Cardiff on Wednesday.)
I'm playing tennis until a quarter past four.

Prepositions of time

at two o'clock
in the afternoon
on Tuesday
on June 17th
I'm playing tennis **until** a quarter past.
I'll ring you back **in** half an hour.
What time does the film start?
(NOT USUALLY 'At what time...')

Suggestions

How about Thursday?
Shall we say Monday morning?

Would like + infinitive

I'd like to make an appointment...
I'd like you to meet my mother.
(NOT I'd like that you meet...)

Take (time)

It'll take a couple of hours at least.
It'll take me a few minutes to shower and get dressed.

This and that

'Who's **that**?' '**This** is Audrey.'

Other structures

I wondered if you were free on Thursday.
I thought you said Tuesday.
Could we make it later?
I'll ring you back.

Words and expressions to learn

couple /'kʌpl/
shower /'ʃaʊə(r)/
diary /'daɪəri/
church /tʃɜːtʃ/
cake /keɪk/
wonder /'wʌndə(r)/
fix /fɪks/
manage /'mænɪdʒ/
practise /'præktɪs/
get changed /'get 'tʃeɪndʒd/
confirm /kən'fɜːm/
It depends. /ɪt dɪ'pendz/
Let me see. /'let mi 'siː/
I'll ring/call you back.
/aɪl 'rɪŋ/'kɔːl ju 'bæk/
say,... /seɪ/
not... either /'nɒt 'aɪðə(r)/
my place /'maɪ 'pleɪs/

Revision vocabulary: do you know these words?

appointment /ə'pɔɪntmənt/
sweater /'swetə(r)/
ironing /'aɪənɪŋ/
mend /mend/
clean /kliːn/
try /traɪ/
free /friː/
early /'ɜːli/
difficult /'dɪfɪkʊlt/
I'm afraid (= 'I'm sorry') /aɪm ə'freɪd/

Unit 7: Lesson A

Grammar and structures

Present perfect tense

I have (I've) broken
you have (you've) broken
he/she/it has ('s) broken
we have (we've) broken
they have (they've) broken

have I broken?
have you broken?
has he/she/it broken?
have we broken?
have they broken?

I have not (haven't) broken
you have not (haven't) broken
he/she/it has not (hasn't) broken
we have not (haven't) broken
they have not (haven't) broken

We use this tense to talk about finished actions, when we are talking about an *unfinished* time period:

Have you **ever** eaten octopus?
I have **often** dreamt of being rich.
During the last three years, I have travelled 100,000 miles.

We do not use the present perfect tense when we talk about a *finished* time period.

When I was a child, I **hated** maths.
    (**NOT** ~~When I was a child, I have hated maths.~~)
I **saw** John **yesterday**.
    (**NOT** ~~I have seen John yesterday.~~)

Present perfect, simple past and simple present

Have you ever...?

PAST ----------- NOW ------------ FUTURE

Did you ever...?   *Do you ever...?*

Have you ever eaten octopus?
When you were a child, **did you ever dream** of being someone else?
Do you ever go out by yourself?

Been (past participle of *go*)

Have you ever **been** to Canada?
I've **been** to Hong Kong twice this year.

Go ... ing

Do you ever **go walking** in the rain?
When you were a child, did you ever **go camping**?

Words and expressions to learn

song /sɒŋ/
job /dʒɒb/
ankle /'æŋkl/
billion /'bɪljən/
boat /bəʊt/
dollar /'dɒlə(r)/
grammar /'græmə(r)/
ice-cream /'aɪs 'kri:m/
advertisement /əd'vɜ:tɪsmənt/
climb /klaɪm/
go camping (went, gone)
    /'gəʊ 'kæmpɪŋ (went, gɒn)/
run away (ran, run)
    /'rʌn ə'weɪ (ræn, rʌn)/
fight (fought, fought) /faɪt (fɔ:t)/
past (adjective) /pɑ:st/
in hospital /ɪn 'hɒspɪtl/
recently /'ri:səntli/
on one occasion /ɒn 'wʌn ə'keɪʒn/

Unit 7: Lesson B

Grammar and structures

Present perfect for news

Police **have arrested** a man in connection with the murder of Professor Bosk.
President Martin **has arrived** for a state visit.
The Minister for Consumer Affairs **has just announced**...
Listen! Something terrible **has just happened**!

Present perfect for changes

The population **has doubled** since 1900.
There used to be two bridges, but one **has fallen** down.

Present perfect progressive

I have been working
you have been working
he/she/it has been working
we have been working
they have been working

have I been working?
have you been working?
etc.

I have not been working
you have not been working
etc.

PAST ---- ---- ---- ---- NOW ------- FUTURE

*It **has been raining** for four weeks.*

I **have been working** all day.
How long **have you been studying** English?
She **has been talking** on the phone since ten o'clock.
    (**NOT** ~~She is talking... since ten o'clock.~~)

Non-progressive verbs

I've **known** her for six weeks.
    (**NOT** ~~I've been knowing her for six weeks.~~)
    (**NOT** ~~I know her for six weeks.~~)
How long **have you had** that car?
She's **been** in America for three months.

140

Since and *for*

I've been here **since April**.
I've been here **for four months**.
 (**NOT** ~~since four months.~~)
They've been talking **since nine
 o'clock**.
They've been talking **for three hours**.

Used to

I **used to** play tennis a lot, but now I
 play football.
 (**NOT** ~~now I use to play football.~~)
I **didn't use to** like classical music.
Did you use to play with dolls when
 you were small?

Pronunciation: /ˈjuːst tə/
(**NOT** ~~/ˈjuːzd tə/~~)

Words and expressions to learn

election /ɪˈlekʃən/
economy /ɪˈkɒnəmi/
president /ˈprezɪdənt/
trip /trɪp/
percentage /pəˈsentɪdʒ/
unemployment /ˌʌnɪmˈplɔɪmənt/
figures /ˈfɪɡəz/
minister /ˈmɪnɪstə(r)/
crops /krɒps/
fruit /fruːt/
silver /ˈsɪlvə(r)/
increase /ɪŋˈkriːs/
sign /saɪn/
improve /ɪmˈpruːv/
average /ˈævrɪdʒ/
abroad /əˈbrɔːd/

Revision vocabulary: do you know these words?

vegetable /ˈvedʒtəbl/
price /praɪs/
population /ˌpɒpjəˈleɪʃn/
rise (rose, risen) /raɪz (rəʊz, rɪzn)/
fall (fell, fallen) /fɔːl (fel, fɔːlən)/
win (won, won) /wɪn (wʌn)/
rain /reɪn/

Unit 8: Lesson A

Grammar and structures

Can for possibility

You **can** (/kn/) get free medical care.
 (**NOT** ~~You can to get...~~)
Where **can** you get a good inexpensive meal?

Will and *may*

Information centres **will** have information about 'bed
 and breakfast'.
If 'bed and breakfast' is too expensive, there **may** be a
 youth hostel nearby.

Connectors

In towns and cities there are buses, **and** in London
 there is...
Fast food shops are cheap, **but** the food is not always
 very good.
The underground is not easy to use, **so** you should learn
 about it before you use it.
Your country may have an agreement with Britain for
 other medical care, **too**;...
There are **also** coaches between some towns and cities;
 these are cheaper than trains.
...a post office. Often **it** is inside a small shop.
People sometimes say 'p' instead of 'pence';
 for example, 'eighty p'.

Words and expressions to learn

campsite /ˈkæmpsaɪt/
fare /feə/
coach /kəʊtʃ/
distance /ˈdɪstəns/
underground /ˈʌndəɡraʊnd/
accident /ˈæksɪdənt/
embassy /ˈembəsi/
consulate /ˈkɒnsələt/
agreement /əˈɡriːmənt/
insurance /ɪnˈʃɔːrəns/
foreign /ˈfɒrən/
at least /ət ˈliːst/
free /friː/
for example /fər ɪɡˈzɑːmpl/
also /ˈɔːlsəʊ/

Revision vocabulary: do you know these words?

pence /pens/
pound /paʊnd/
hotel /həʊˈtel/
youth hostel /ˈjuːθ ˈhɒstl/
train /treɪn/

bus /bʌs/
family /ˈfæməli/
only /ˈəʊnli/
post office /ˈpəʊst ˈɒfɪs/
stamp /stæmp/
village /ˈvɪlɪdʒ/
town /taʊn/
shop /ʃɒp/
restaurant /ˈrestrənt/
food /fuːd/
meal /miːl/
pub /pʌb/
country /ˈkʌntri/
journey /ˈdʒɜːni/
health /helθ/
change (verb) /tʃeɪndʒ/
stay /steɪ/
help /help/
buy (bought, bought) /baɪ (bɔːt)/
need /niːd/
sometimes /ˈsʌmtaɪmz/
usually /ˈjuːʒəli/
often /ˈɒfn/
always /ˈɔːlweɪz/
cheap /tʃiːp/
expensive /ɪkˈspensɪv/

Unit 8: Lesson B

Grammar and structures

Should and *will have to*

You **should take** sunglasses.
 (**NOT** ~~You should to take...~~)
You'll **have to** have a visa.

Words and expressions to learn

operator /ˈɒpəreɪtə(r)/
airline /ˈeəlaɪn/
wallet /ˈwɒlɪt/
passport /ˈpɑːspɔːt/
customs /ˈkʌstəmz/
pickpocket /ˈpɪkpɒkɪt/
competition /ˌkɒmpəˈtɪʃn/
choice /tʃɔɪs/
pick up /ˈpɪk ˈʌp/
cancel /ˈkænsl/
go through customs (went, gone) /ˈɡəʊ ˈθruː ˈkʌstəmz (went, ɡɒn)/
reverse-charge call /rɪˈvɜːs ˈtʃɑːdʒ ˈkɔːl/
collect call (American) /kəˈlekt ˈkɔːl/

STD code /ˈes ˈtiː ˈdiː ˈkəʊd/
area code (American) /ˈeərɪə ˈkəʊd/
immigration control /ˌɪmɪˈɡreɪʃn kənˈtrəʊl/

Revision vocabulary: do you know these words?

likely /ˈlaɪkli/
easy /ˈiːzi/
light /laɪt/
exciting /ɪkˈsaɪtɪŋ/
tired /ˈtaɪəd/
beautiful /ˈbjuːtɪfl/
sunny /ˈsʌni/
comfortable /ˈkʌmftəbl/

Unit 9: Lesson A

Grammar and structures

Present perfect and simple past

The present perfect tense is used to tell people about very recent past events which are 'news'. If you find a box of chocolates on your desk you can say:

Someone **has left** me a box of chocolates!
    (NOT Someone left me...)

The simple past is used to talk about past events which are completely finished, and which are not 'news'. Compare:

My son **has** just **fallen** off a wall. I think he **has broken** his leg.
When I was ten, I **fell** off a wall and **broke** my leg.

Remember: we do not use the present perfect with 'finished-time' words.

Some of the demonstrators **left** home shortly after midnight last night.
    (NOT ... have left home shortly after midnight...)

There has been

There's been an accident.

Words and expressions to learn

fire /'faɪə(r)/
neighbour /'neɪbə(r)/
kitchen /'kɪtʃɪn/
burglary /'bɜːgləri/
smoke /sməʊk/
window /'wɪndəʊ/
instructions /ɪn'strʌkʃənz/
ambulance /'æmbjʊləns/
emergency /ɪ'mɜːdʒənsi/
bleed (bled, bled) /bliːd (bled)/

steal (stole, stolen) /stiːl (stəʊl, 'stəʊlən)/
cover /'kʌvə(r)/

Unit 9: Lesson B

Grammar and structures

Make + object + adjective
Chocolate **makes you fat.**

Make + object + infinitive without *to*
Rain **makes the flowers grow.**
    (NOT ... makes the flowers to grow.)

Making apologies
I'm sorry. I didn't mean to do it.
I didn't mean to.
I was thinking about something else.
I forgot what I was doing.
It was an accident.
I didn't do it on purpose.

Accepting apologies
That's all right.
It doesn't matter.
It wasn't your fault.

Words and expressions to learn
cough /kɒf/
switch /swɪtʃ/
brake /breɪk/
kiss /kɪs/
mean (meant, meant) /miːn (ment)/
see (saw, seen) (= understand) /siː (sɔː, siːn)/
burn (burnt, burnt) /bɜːn (bɜːnt)/
It doesn't matter. /ɪt 'dʌznt 'mætə(r)/
That's all right. /'ðæts 'ɔːl 'raɪt/
my/your fault /'maɪ/'jɔː 'fɔːlt/
on purpose /ɒn 'pɜːpəs/
than usual /ðən 'juːʒuːʊl/

Learn two or more of these:
accelerator /ək'seləreɪtə(r)/
row /raʊ/
control /kən'trəʊl/
sigh /saɪ/

Revision vocabulary: do you know these words?
rain /reɪn/
chocolate /'tʃɒklət/
forget (forgot, forgotten) /fə'get (fə'gɒt, fə'gɒtn)/
jump /dʒʌmp/
get (got, got) /get (gɒt)/
crash /kræʃ/
lorry /'lɒri/
careful /'keəfl/
else /els/
actually /'æktʃəli/
because /bɪ'kɒz/
so /səʊ/

Unit 10: Lesson A

Grammar and structures

If
If you are travelling at 80kph in a car, you can stop safely in 52m.
If your ancestors' language was Choctaw, they lived in America.
If today is your golden wedding anniversary, you have been married for 50 years.

Special case: *if* + present for future idea
If you **see** a black cat you'**ll have** good luck.
    (NOT If you will see...)
What **will happen if** John **speaks** to the girl?
    (NOT if John will speak...)

If and *when*
When I go to bed tonight, I'll...
    (I *will* go to bed.)
If I go to Scotland, I'll...
    (I *may* go to Scotland.)

Negative imperatives; imperatives with *if*
Don't look at the teacher.
If today is Tuesday, **write** the number 12. **If not, don't write** anything.

Words and expressions to learn

score /skɔ:(r)/
wedding /'wedɪŋ/
great-grandparents
   /'greɪt 'grænpeərənts/
century /'sentʃəri/
island /'aɪlənd/
superstition /su:pə'stɪʃn/
luck /lʌk/

shoulder /'ʃəʊldə(r)/
hat /hæt/
New Year /'nju: 'jɪə(r)/
spill (spilt, spilt) /spɪl (spɪlt)/
itch /ɪtʃ/
close /kləʊz/
drunk /drʌŋk/
safely /'seɪfli/

Revision vocabulary: do you know these words?

language /'læŋgwɪdʒ/
cat /kæt/
wine /waɪn/
salt /sɔ:lt/
umbrella /ʌm'brelə/
mirror /'mɪrə(r)/
travel /'trævl/

throw (threw, thrown)
   /θrəʊ (θru:, θrəʊn)/
open /'əʊpn/
break (broke, broken)
   /breɪk (brəʊk, 'brəʊkn)/
hit (hit, hit) /hɪt/
dark /dɑ:k/

Unit 10: Lesson B

Grammar and structures

Present tense with future meaning

When you **do** this, the cat will run.
   (**NOT** When you will do this, ...)
As soon as the kettle **is** full, move the fish.
Turn the small wheel **until** the kettle **is** under the tap.

When and *until*

When a melon is ready to eat, the end opposite the
   stem will be fairly soft.
Onions won't make you cry **until** they lose their roots.

Remember: *until* can also be used with days, dates,
times, etc.

She'll be there **until** half past six.

Words and expressions to learn

tap /tæp/
tin /tɪn/
fridge /frɪdʒ/
knife (knives) /naɪf (naɪvz)/
butter /'bʌtə(r)/
onion /'ʌnjən/
turn on/off /'tɜ:n 'ɒn/'ɒf/

fill /fɪl/
cry /kraɪ/
full /fʊl/
sharp /ʃɑ:p/
hard /hɑ:d/
last /lɑ:st/

Learn three or more of these:	
kettle /'ketl/	peel /pi:l/
string /strɪŋ/	pour /pɔ:(r)/
hook /hʊk/	spring /sprɪŋ/
bell /bel/	tap (verb) /tæp/
stem /stem/	bubble /'bʌbl/
root /ru:t/	shrink (shrank, shrunk)
skin /skɪn/	/ʃrɪŋk (ʃræŋk, ʃrʌŋk)/
needle /'ni:dl/	

THERE IS NO SUMMARY FOR UNIT 11, LESSON A

Unit 11: Lesson B

Words and expressions to learn

experience /ɪks'pɪərɪəns/
salary /'sæləri/
interview /'ɪntəvju:/
canteen /kæn'ti:n/
conditions /kən'dɪʃənz/

Managing Director /'mænɪdʒɪŋ də'rektə(r)/
qualifications /kwɒlɪfɪ'keɪʃənz/
advertise /'ædvətaɪz/
apply /ə'plaɪ/
essential /ɪ'senʃʊl/

full-time /'fʊl 'taɪm/
Yours faithfully /'jɔ:z 'feɪθfʊli/
Yours sincerely /'jɔ:z sɪn'sɪəli/
look forward /'lʊk 'fɔ:wəd/
I look forward to hearing from you.
as soon as possible /əz 'su:n əz 'pɒsəbl/

Additional material

Lesson 7A, Exercise 1

Brighton in the Rain

I've never been to Athens and I've never been to Rome
I've only seen the Pyramids in picture books at home
I've never sailed across the sea or been inside a plane
I've always spent my holidays in Brighton in the rain.

I've never eaten foreign food or drunk in a foreign bar
I've never kissed a foreign girl or driven a foreign car
I've never had to find my way in a country I don't know
I've always known just where I am and where I'll never go.

I've read travel books by writers who have been to Pakistan
I've heard people telling stories of adventures in Iran
I've watched TV documentaries about China and Brazil
But I've never been abroad myself; it's making me feel ill.

I've studied several languages like Hindi and Malay
I've learnt lots of useful sentences I've never been able to say
The furthest place I've ever been was to the Isle of Man
And that was full of tourists from Jamaica and Japan.

I've never been to Athens and I've never been to Rome
I've only seen the Pyramids in picture books at home
I've never sailed across the sea or been inside a plane
I've always spent my holidays in Brighton in the rain.

Jonathan Dykes (lyrics)
Robert Campbell (music)

Lesson 9B, Exercise 7

You Made Me Love You

You made me love you
I didn't wanna do it
I didn't wanna do it
You made me love you
And all the time you knew it
I guess you always knew it.
You made me happy, sometimes
You made me glad
But there were times when
You made me feel so sad.

You made me sigh, 'cause
I didn't wanna tell you
I didn't wanna tell you
I think you're grand, that's true,
Yes I do, 'deed I do, you know I do
Gimme, gimme, gimme, gimme
What I cry for
You know you've got the kind of kisses
That I'd die for
You know you made me love you.

(Monaco and McCarthy)

Lesson 10A, Exercise 8

Song for a Rainy Sunday

It's a rainy Sunday morning and I don't know what to do
If I stay in bed all day, I'll only think about you
If I try to study, I won't learn anything new
And if I go for a walk on my own in the park,
I'll probably catch the flu!

I just don't know (He doesn't know)
What to do (What to do)
I just don't know (He doesn't know)
What to do (What to do)

If I stay in bed all day, I'll only think about you
If I try to study, I won't learn anything new
And if I go for a walk on my own in the park,
I'll probably catch the flu – atchoo!

It's nearly Sunday lunchtime and I don't know where to eat
If I walk to the fish and chip shop, I'll only get wet feet
If I stay at home for lunch, I'll have to eat last week's meat
And if I get in my car and drive to the pub, I probably won't
   get a seat

I just don't know (He doesn't know)
Where to eat (Where to eat)
I just don't know (He doesn't know)
Where to eat (Where to eat)

If I walk to the fish and chip shop, I'll only get wet feet
If I stay at home for lunch, I'll have to eat last week's meat
And if I get in my car and drive to the pub, I probably won't
   get a seat

The rain has stopped and I'd like to go out
But I don't know where to go
If I invite you out for a drink, you'll probably say no
If I go to the theatre alone, I won't enjoy the show
And if I stay here at home on my own, I'll be bored and
   miserable, so

I just don't know (He doesn't know)
Where to go (Where to go)
I just don't know (He doesn't know)
Where to go (Where to go)

If I invite you out for a drink, you'll probably say no
If I go to the theatre alone, I won't enjoy the show
And if I stay here at home on my own, I'll be bored and
   miserable, so

I'm going to the theatre but I don't know what to wear
I know if I look through my socks I'll never find a pair
If I put on my new green boots people will probably stare
And if my tie isn't straight and they complain 'cause I'm late,
I'll say, 'Listen, mate: I don't care!'

I just don't care (He doesn't care)
What I wear (Life isn't fair)
I just don't care (He doesn't care)
What I wear (Life isn't fair)

I know if I look through my socks I'll never find a pair
If I put on my new green boots people will probably stare
And if my tie isn't straight and they complain 'cause I'm late,
I'll say, 'Listen, mate: I don't care!'

Jonathan Dykes (lyrics)
Robert Campbell (music)

Acknowledgements

The authors and publishers are grateful to the following copyright owners for permission to reproduce photographs, illustrations, texts and music. Every endeavour has been made to contact copyright owners and apologies are expressed for any omissions.

page 21: Reproduced by permission of Syndication International. page 31: Reproduced by permission of *Punch.* page 39: Reproduced by permission of British Telecom. page 60: *cl* 'My mother said . . .' from *God Bless Love*, Nanette Newman (Collins, 1972), © Invalid Children's Association, reproduced by kind permission of ICA. *tc, br* 'Dear God . . .', 'If they don't want . . .' from *Children's Letters to God* (Fontana, Collins, 1976), reproduced by permission of the Publisher. *cr* 'My mum only likes . . .' from Extracts from Nanette Newman's Collections of Sayings, by permission of the authors, © reserved. page 61: From Extracts from Nanette Newman's Collection of Sayings, by permission of the authors, © reserved. page 92: *tr* Courtesy of John, Hairdresser, Croydon, *cr* Mobil Oil Company Limited. page 93: *tr* Courtesy of Joan Galleli, The Shirley Poppy. page 96: *b* Reproduced by permission of *Punch.* page 98: From the *Longman Active Study Dictionary of English* edited by Della Summers, Longman 1983. page 102: *tr* Photographie Musée National d'Art Moderne, Centre Georges Pompidou, Paris. *tl* Reproduced by courtesy of the Trustees, The National Gallery, London. *bl* Reproduced by courtesy of the Board of Trustees of the Victoria and Albert Museum. page 104: *l* Courtesy of Gallery Lingard. *r* Reproduced from the poster of the London Mozart Players 1984–1985. *c* Reproduced from London Features International Ltd. page 113: From an article by Anna Tomforde in the *Guardian* – adapted. page 115: Reproduced by permission of *Punch.* page 116: *t* Reproduced by permission of *Punch.* *b* From *Weekend Book of Jokes* 21 (Harmsworth Publications Ltd.), reproduced by permission of Associated Newspapers Plc. page 117: Reproduced by permission of Syndication International. page 124: 'My dad . . .', 'A prime minister . . .' 'When you grow up . . .' Reproduced by permission of Bryan Forbes Ltd. page 128: Nos. 1-7, 10 from *The Highway Code* (Her Majesty's Stationery Office), Reproduced by permission of the Publisher. Colour details: 1. green light showing. Other lights are red (top) and amber (middle). 2. same as (1) except that red light is showing. 3. red triangle, white background, black letters. 4. white circle, red background, white horizontal line. 5. red circle and diagonal, white background, black directional sign. 6. red circle, white background, black man. 7. red triangle, white background, black car and lines. 8. grey road, yellow double lines, white dotted lines. 9. grey road, white lines. 10. red triangle, white background, black rocks. page 131: *tl* McLachlan. *tr, c, bl* Reproduced by permission of *Punch.* *br* Reproduced by permission of Syndication International. page 156: Song *You Made Me Love You*, lyrics: Joe McCarthy, music: James V. Monaco. © 1913 Broadway Music Corp, USA. Sub-published by Francis Day & Hunter Ltd., London WC2H 0LD. Reproduced by permission of EMI Music Publishing Ltd. and International Music Publications. page 158: Song *Trying to Love Two Women*, by Sonny Throckmorton, © Cross Keys Publishing Company Inc., USA. Sub-published by EMI Music Publishing Ltd., London WC2H 0LD. Reproduced by permission of EMI Publishing Ltd. and International Music Publications. page 158: Song *The Riddle Song* by Harry Robinson & Julie Felix, © 1965 TRO Essex Music Ltd., Bury Place, London WC1A 2LA for the World International Copyright secured. All Rights Reserved. page 159: The version of the song *Logger Lover* is by Dick Stephenson and is used with permission. page 159: *What Did You Learn in School Today?*, words and music by Tom Paxton. Reprinted by permission of Harmony Music Limited, 19/20 Poland Street, London W1V 3DD.

The songs *Brighton in the Rain* (Lesson 7A, page 156), *Song for a Rainy Sunday* (Lesson 10A, page 156), *The Island* (Lesson 13A, page 156), *My Old Dad* (Lesson 14A, page 59), *Another Street Incident* (Lesson 17B, page 72), and *A Bigger Heart* (Lesson 22A, page 90) were specially written for *The Cambridge English Course* Book 2 by Jonathan Dykes (lyrics) and Robert Campbell (music). The recorded material for Lesson 11A, Exercise 4 (page 181) and Revision Tests 1 (page 166) and 2 (page 170) is used by kind permission of Wiltshire Radio.

Ace Photo Agency: p92 *l*. BBC Hulton Picture Library: p110 *br*. Camera Press Limited: p110 *tr*, nos. 2, 3, *c* (Margaret Thatcher), *b* (second from *l*). The Daily Telegraph: pages 98 *l*, 122 (teacher, farmer, 3 industrial photos). p50: *tc* Courtesy of Jaakko Poyry (UK) Limited. London Features International Limited: p104 *c*. Monitor Picture Library: p93 *tl, br*. Pictorial Press Limited: p110 *b* (second from *r*). Alan Philip: pages 6–7, 36, 64. The Press Association: p95 *t*. Doc Rowe: p105. Spectrum Colour Library: pages 36–37, 98 *r*. Sporting Pictures UK Limited: p95 *b*. Syndication International Limited: pages 110 *tc, cr*, nos. 1, 4, *bl*, 122 (housewife, nurse). John Topham Picture Library: pages 68, 74–75. p125: © United Kingdom Atomic Energy Authority, used with permission. Reg van Cuÿlenburg: pages 22, 63, 66–67. Catherine Walter: p8. Wiggins Teape Group: p50 *tr, br*. Jason Youé: pages 92 *tr, cr*, 93 *tr, cl, cr*, 125 *t*.

John Craddock: Malcolm Barter, pages 14 *t*, 37 *b*, 38–39, 58, 69 *b*, 78–79, 80–81; Alexa Rutherford, pages 20, 28, 59, 94, 108 *t*, 120; Kate Simunek, p57; Ian Fleming and Associates Limited: Terry Burton, p100; David Lewis Management: Odette Buchanan, pages 18, 45, 91, 112; Bob Harvey, pages 40, 41 *r*, 65, 69 *t*, 72, 88, 113, 121 *t*; Jon Miller, pages 10–11, 84, 121 *b*; Linda Rogers: Mike Whittlesea, pages 27, 44 *b*, 71 *l*, 82 *t*, 108 *b*, 114 *t*; Linden Artists Limited: Jon Davis, pages 30 *b*, 35, 70, 126–127; Val Sangster, pages 16, 24, 71 *r*, 96 *t*, 114 *b*.

Paul Davenport, pages 44 *t*, 52–53, 76; Paul Francis, pages 14 *b*, 15; Martin Gordon, p42; Gary Inwood, pages 41 *l*, 43, 73, 82 *b*, 121; Jane Molineaux, pages 26, 77; Chris Rawlings, pages 30 *t*, 33; Nik Spender, pages 12–13, 56, 83, 118, 132–133; Tony Streek, pages 23, 34, 54 *t*, 89, 119; Malcolm Ward, pages 19, 54 *b*, 86, 109, 111; Jack Wood, pages 51, 54 *b*, 55, 112; Mike Woodhatch, pages 106–107; John Youé & Associates.

(Abbreviations: *t*=top *b*=bottom *c*=centre *r*=right *l*=left)

Phonetic symbols

Vowels

symbol	example	symbol	example
/iː/	eat /iːt/	/eɪ/	day /deɪ/
/i/	happy /'hæpi/	/aɪ/	my /maɪ/
/ɪ/	it /ɪt/	/ɔɪ/	boy /bɔɪ/
/e/	when /wen/	/aʊ/	now /naʊ/
/æ/	cat /kæt/	/əʊ/	go /gəʊ/
/ɑː/	hard /hɑːd/	/ɪə/	here /hɪə(r)/
/ɒ/	not /nɒt/	/eə/	chair /tʃeə(r)/
/ɔː/	sort /sɔːt/; all /ɔːl/	/ʊə/	tour /tʊə(r)/
/ʊ/	look /lʊk/		
/uː/	too /tuː/		
/ʌ/	up /ʌp/		
/ɜː/	bird /bɜːd/; turn /tɜːn/		
/ə/	about /ə'baʊt/; mother /'mʌðə(r)/		

Consonants

symbol	example	symbol	example
/p/	pen /pen/	/h/	who /huː/; how /haʊ/
/b/	big /bɪg/	/m/	meet /miːt/
/t/	two /tuː/	/n/	no /nəʊ/
/d/	do /duː/	/ŋ/	sing /sɪŋ/
/k/	look /lʊk/; cup /kʌp/	/l/	long /lɒŋ/
/g/	get /get/	/r/	right /raɪt/
/tʃ/	China /'tʃaɪnə/	/j/	yet /jet/
/dʒ/	Japan /dʒə'pæn/	/w/	will /wɪl/
/f/	fall /fɔːl/		
/v/	very /'veri/		
/θ/	think /θɪŋk/		
/ð/	then /ðen/		
/s/	see /siː/		
/z/	zoo /zuː/; is /ɪz/		
/ʃ/	shoe /ʃuː/		
/ʒ/	pleasure /'pleʒə(r)/; decision /dɪ'sɪʒn/		

Stress

Stress is shown by a mark (') in front of the stressed syllable.

mother /'mʌðə(r)/
about /ə'baʊt/
China /'tʃaɪnə/
Japan /dʒə'pæn/

Irregular verbs

Infinitive	Simple Past	Past Participle
be /biː/	was /wəz, wɒz/; were /wə, wɜː(r)/	been /bɪn, biːn/
beat /biːt/	beat /biːt/	beaten /'biːtn/
become /bɪ'kʌm/	became /bɪ'keɪm/	become /bɪ'kʌm/
begin /bɪ'gɪn/	began /bɪ'gæn/	begun /bɪ'gʌn/
bend /bend/	bent /bent/	bent /bent/
bet /bet/	bet /bet/	bet /bet/
bite /baɪt/	bit /bɪt/	bitten /'bɪtn/
bleed /bliːd/	bled /bled/	bled /bled/
break /breɪk/	broke /brəʊk/	broken /'brəʊkn/
bring /brɪŋ/	brought /brɔːt/	brought /brɔːt/
build /bɪld/	built /bɪlt/	built /bɪlt/
burn /bɜːn/	burnt /bɜːnt/	burnt /bɜːnt/
buy /baɪ/	bought /bɔːt/	bought /bɔːt/
catch /kætʃ/	caught /kɔːt/	caught /kɔːt/
choose /tʃuːz/	chose /tʃəʊz/	chosen /'tʃəʊzn/
come /kʌm/	came /keɪm/	come /kʌm/
cost /kɒst/	cost /kɒst/	cost /kɒst/
cut /kʌt/	cut /kʌt/	cut /kʌt/
deal /diːl/	dealt /delt/	dealt /delt/
do /dʊ, də, duː/	did /dɪd/	done /dʌn/
draw /drɔː/	drew /druː/	drawn /drɔːn/
dream /driːm/	dreamt /dremt/	dreamt /dremt/
drink /drɪŋk/	drank /dræŋk/	drunk /drʌŋk/
drive /draɪv/	drove /drəʊv/	driven /'drɪvn/
eat /iːt/	ate /et/	eaten /'iːtn/
fall /fɔːl/	fell /fel/	fallen /'fɔːlən/
feel /fiːl/	felt /felt/	felt /felt/
find /faɪnd/	found /faʊnd/	found /faʊnd/
fly /flaɪ/	flew /fluː/	flown /fləʊn/
forget /fə'get/	forgot /fə'gɒt/	forgotten /fə'gɒtn/
get /get/	got /gɒt/	got /gɒt/
give /gɪv/	gave /geɪv/	given /'gɪvn/
go /gəʊ/	went /went/	gone /gɒn/; been /bɪn, biːn/
grow /grəʊ/	grew /gruː/	grown /grəʊn/
have /həv, hæv/	had /(h)əd, hæd/	had /hæd/
hear /hɪə(r)/	heard /hɜːd/	heard /hɜːd/
hide /haɪd/	hid /hɪd/	hidden /'hɪdn/
hit /hɪt/	hit /hɪt/	hit /hɪt/
hurt /hɜːt/	hurt /hɜːt/	hurt /hɜːt/
keep /kiːp/	kept /kept/	kept /kept/
know /nəʊ/	knew /njuː/	known /nəʊn/
lead /liːd/	led /led/	led /led/
learn /lɜːn/	learnt /lɜːnt/	learnt /lɜːnt/
leave /liːv/	left /left/	left /left/
lend /lend/	lent /lent/	lent /lent/
let /let/	let /let/	let /let/
lie /laɪ/	lay /leɪ/	lain /leɪn/
lose /luːz/	lost /lɒst/	lost /lɒst/
make /meɪk/	made /meɪd/	made /meɪd/
mean /miːn/	meant /ment/	meant /ment/
meet /miːt/	met /met/	met /met/
pay /peɪ/	paid /peɪd/	paid /peɪd/
put /pʊt/	put /pʊt/	put /pʊt/
read /riːd/	read /red/	read /red/
rewind /riː'waɪnd/	rewound /riː'waʊnd/	rewound /riː'waʊnd/
ride /raɪd/	rode /rəʊd/	ridden /'rɪdn/
ring /rɪŋ/	rang /ræŋ/	rung /rʌŋ/
rise /raɪz/	rose /rəʊz/	risen /'rɪzn/
run /rʌn/	ran /ræn/	run /rʌn/
say /seɪ/	said /sed/	said /sed/
see /siː/	saw /sɔː/	seen /siːn/
sell /sel/	sold /səʊld/	sold /səʊld/
send /send/	sent /sent/	sent /sent/
shake /ʃeɪk/	shook /ʃʊk/	shaken /'ʃeɪkn/
show /ʃəʊ/	showed /ʃəʊd/	shown /ʃəʊn/
shrink /ʃrɪŋk/	shrank /ʃræŋk/	shrunk /ʃrʌŋk/
shut /ʃʌt/	shut /ʃʌt/	shut /ʃʌt/
sing /sɪŋ/	sang /sæŋ/	sung /sʌŋ/
sit /sɪt/	sat /sæt/	sat /sæt/
sleep /sliːp/	slept /slept/	slept /slept/
smell /smel/	smelt /smelt/	smelt /smelt/
speak /spiːk/	spoke /spəʊk/	spoken /'spəʊkn/
spell /spel/	spelt /spelt/	spelt /spelt/
spend /spend/	spent /spent/	spent /spent/
spill /spɪl/	spilt /spɪlt/	spilt /spɪlt/
stand /stænd/	stood /stʊd/	stood /stʊd/
steal /stiːl/	stole /stəʊl/	stolen /'stəʊlən/
stick /stɪk/	stuck /stʌk/	stuck /stʌk/
swim /swɪm/	swam /swæm/	swum /swʌm/
take /teɪk/	took /tʊk/	taken /'teɪkn/
teach /tiːtʃ/	taught /tɔːt/	taught /tɔːt/
tell /tel/	told /təʊld/	told /təʊld/
think /θɪŋk/	thought /θɔːt/	thought /θɔːt/
throw /θrəʊ/	threw /θruː/	thrown /θrəʊn/
understand /ʌndə'stænd/	understood /ʌndə'stʊd/	understood /ʌndə'stʊd/
wake up /'weɪk 'ʌp/	woke up /'wəʊk 'ʌp/	woken up /'wəʊkn 'ʌp/
wear /weə(r)/	wore /wɔː(r)/	worn /wɔːn/
win /wɪn/	won /wʌn/	won /wʌn/
wind /waɪnd/	wound /waʊnd/	wound /waʊnd/
write /raɪt/	wrote /rəʊt/	written /'rɪtn/